ISBN 0-8373-6646-1

DANTES– **46**

Rudman's Question and Answers on the

DANTES
SUBJECT STANDARDIZED TESTS

Subject Examination In ...

PRINCIPLES OF
FINANCE

Questions and Answers

NATIONAL LEARNING CORPORATION
212 MICHAEL DRIVE, SYOSSET, NEW YORK 11791 (516) 921-8888

Copyright © 2005 by

National Learning Corporation

212 Michael Drive, Syosset, New York 11791

(516) 921-8888
Outside N.Y.: 1(800) 645-6337
ORDER FAX: 1(516) 921-8743
www.passbooks.com
email: passbooks @ aol.com
sales @ passbooks.com
info @ passbooks.com

PRINTED IN THE UNITED STATES OF AMERICA

PASSBOOK®

NOTICE

PASSBOOK SERIES®

THE *PASSBOOK SERIES®* has been created to prepare applicants and candidates for the ultimate academic battlefield—the examination room.

At some time in our lives, each and every one of us may be required to take an examination—for validation, matriculation, admission, qualification, registration, certification, or licensure.

Based on the assumption that every applicant or candidate has met the basic formal educational standards, has taken the required number of courses, and read the necessary texts, the *PASSBOOK SERIES®* furnishes the one special preparation which may assure passing with confidence, instead of failing with insecurity. Examination questions—together with answers—are furnished as the basic vehicle for study so that the mysteries of the examination and its compounding difficulties may be eliminated or diminished by a sure method.

This book is meant to help you pass your examination provided that you qualify and are serious in your objective.

The entire field is reviewed through the huge store of content information which is succinctly presented through a provocative and challenging approach—the question-and-answer method.

A climate of success is established by furnishing the correct answers at the end of each test.

You soon learn to recognize types of questions, forms of questions, and patterns of questioning. You may even begin to anticipate expected outcomes.

You perceive that many questions are repeated or adapted so that you gain acute insights, which may enable you to score many sure points.

You learn how to confront new questions, or types of questions, and to attack them confidently and work out the correct answers.

You note objectives and emphases, and recognize pitfalls and dangers, so that you may make positive educational adjustments.

Moreover, you are kept fully informed in relation to new concepts, methods, practices, and directions in the field.

You discover that you are actually taking the examination all the time: you are preparing for the examination by "taking" an examination, not by reading extraneous and/or supererogatory textbooks.

In short, this PASSBOOK®, used directedly, should be an important factor in helping you to pass your test.

DANTES Subject Standardized Tests

INTRODUCTION

The DANTES (Defense Activity for Non-Traditional Education Support) subject standardized tests are comprehensive college and graduate level examinations given by the Armed Forces, colleges and graduate schools as end-of-subject course evaluation final examinations or to obtain college equivalency credits in the various subject areas tested.

Active military personnel may take CLEP (College-Level Examination Program) examinations without charge through the DANTES program. Information about DANTES and CLEP may be obtained from the Test Control Officers at military installations, and from Educational Testing Service in Princeton, New Jersey.

The DANTES Examination Program enables students to obtain college credit for what they have learned on the job, through self-study, personal interest, correspondence courses or by any other means. It is used by colleges and universities to award college credit to students who demonstrate that they know as much as students completing an equivalent college course. It is a cost-efficient, time-saving way for students to use their knowledge to accomplish their educational goals.

Most schools accept the American Council on Education (ACE) recommendations for the minimum score required and the amount of credit awarded, but not all schools do. Be sure to check the policy regarding the score level required for credit and the number of credits to be awarded.

Not all tests are accepted by all institutions. Even when a test is accepted by an institution, it may not be acceptable for every program at that institution. Before considering testing, ascertain the acceptability of a specific test for a particular course.

Colleges and universities that administer DANTES tests may administer them to any applicant -- or they may administer the tests only to students registered at their institution. Decisions about who will be allowed to test are made by the school. Students should contact the test center to determine current policies and schedules for DANTES testing.

Colleges and universities authorized to administer DANTES tests usually do so throughout the calendar year. Each school sets its own fee for test administration and establishes its own testing schedule. Contact the representative at the administering school directly to make arrangements for testing.

Your Experience Can Earn You Credit.

It's a fact. People learn in many ways . . . through hobbies . . . interests . . . reading . . . work. The DANTES Program is a way for you to "cash in" on what you've learned from *your* experiences.

Take advantage of DANTES tests to earn college credit for what you know. More than 30 subjects are offered. There are bound to be areas where your knowledge can pay off academically.

Here are just a few of the program's benefits for you:

- *Time and Money Saver*
  You don't have to sit through classes and pay for courses when you already know most of what's being taught and can learn the rest yourself.

- *Credits Widely Accepted*
  Hundreds of colleges nationwide now give credit for DANTES tests. And the list is growing!

- *Quicker Route to the Degree*
  Your dreams are a little closer than you thought possible. With DANTES.

- *Start Fast*
  No need to wait to take advanced courses. Passing DANTES tests gives you a real head start.

Sound Good? Here's How to Get Going!

Check with your college to see if it administers the DANTES program. If the college doesn't but would like to, ask that someone **call collect** (609-951-1756) or write to the DANTES Program Office (see address below).

If you find that your college *accepts* DANTES credits, but does not *administer* the tests, here's what you do —

- Write to the DANTES Program Office for a list of colleges that administer the test. Chances are there's one nearby.

- Call any of the ETS Regional Offices (Tucker, GA; Oakland, CA; Evanston, IL; Phoenix, AZ; and Princeton, NJ. DANTES tests are given at all of those locations.

- In the military or in the reserves? DoD employees and family members may be able to take DANTES tests at a Military Education Office or Navy Campus Office.

Check Out the DANTES Test List.

Match the titles with the things you have learned. Consider how much college credit you might gain by taking some DANTES tests.

Your college should have fact sheets with more information about each DANTES test. If not, please write to us directly, or e-mail us at dantes@chauncey.com. Tell us which subjects interest you.

——————————————▶

**DANTES Program Office
Educational Testing Service
Princeton, NJ 08541-0001**

from the official announcement for instructional purposes

MATHEMATICS

Introductory College Algebra
- Functions and graphs
- Fundamental algebraic operations
- Linear equations, inequalities, word problems
- Radicals and exponents

Principles of Statistics
- Descriptive statistics
- Correlation, regression, probability
- Chance models, sampling, test of significance

SOCIAL SCIENCE

Art of the Western World
- Greece and Rome
- Romanesque and Gothic
- Renaissance
- Baroque, rococo, neoclassicism, romanticism
- Twentieth century

The Civil War and Reconstruction
- Causes of the war
- Political situations and the war between 1861 and 1865
- Reconstruction

Contemporary Western Europe
- Historical background
- Political systems
- Societal issues
- Integration

Criminal Justice
- Criminal behavior
- Police and criminal justice system
- Court system
- Corrections

Drug and Alcohol Abuse
- Pharmacological principles
- Classification of drugs
- Properties of alcohol, sedative hypnotics, narcotic analgesics, stimulants, hallucinogens and other drugs
- Prevention/treatment

Foundations of Education
- Contemporary issues in education
- Past and current influences on education
- Interrelationships between contemporary issues and influences, past or current, in education

Fundamentals of Counseling
- Counselor roles and functions
- Counseling relationships
- Theoretical approaches
- Social and cultural foundations

General Anthropology
- Anthropology branches, methodologies, and theoretical perspectives
- Physical anthropology and archeology
- Nature of culture
- Social, economic, political, and religious organization

A History of the Vietnam War
- The first Vietnam War (1945-1954)
- LBJ goes to war (1964-1965)
- Tet Offensive (1968)
- Vietnamizing the war (1968-1973)
- Peace is at hand (1968-1973)

Human/Cultural Geography
- Basic facts and concepts
- Culture and environment
- Spatial processes
- Regional geography

Introduction to Law Enforcement
- U.S. criminal justice and police systems
- Issues and organization of police
- Constitutional law and precedents

Introduction to the Modern Middle East
- Geography and early history
- Nineteenth and early twentieth century
- First and Second World wars
- Soviet-U.S. rivalry, Suez Crisis, Iranian Revolution, Persian Gulf Crisis

Lifespan Developmental Psychology
- Biological development
- Perception, learning, and memory
- Social, emotional, and personality development
- Cognition and language

BUSINESS

Business Law II
- Sales of goods
- Debtor and creditor relations
- Business organizations
- Property
- Commercial paper

Business Mathematics
- Basic computation — fractions, percents, ratios, graphs
- Business applications

Introduction to Business
- Economic, international, government, and ownership issues
- Management process
- Human resources and production
- Marketing, finance

Introduction to Computers with Programming in BASIC
- Hardware, software, data management
- Communications and connectivity
- BASIC: I/O, expressions, loops, conditionals, strings, arrays

Management Information Systems
- Systems theory, analysis and design of systems
- Hardware and software
- Database management
- Telecommunications
- Management of the MIS functional area, informational support

Money and Banking
- Role of commercial banks and other intermediaries
- Federal Reserve System
- Macroeconomic activity, U.S. policy, international system

Personal Finance
- Financial goals, budgeting, cash management, economic terminology
- Credit, debt, and major purchases
- Taxes and insurance
- Investments, retirement and estate planning

Personnel/Human Resource Management
- Employment actions
- Training and development
- Performance appraisals
- Compensation and personnel legislation
- Labor relations

Principles of Finance
- Financial statements and ratio analysis
- Capital budgeting
- Time value of money
- Break-even and leverage, common stock

Principles of Financial Accounting
- General concepts and principles
- Financial statements
- Accruals and deferrals
- Current accounts

Principles of Supervision
- Roles and responsibilities
- Management functions
- Legal issues, stress management, unions, productivity and quality concerns

Organizational Behavior
- Individual and group processes and characteristics
- Organizational processes and behavior
- Change and development processes

APPLIED TECHNOLOGY

Technical Writing
- Elements of technical reports
- Style, grammar, mechanics, organizing
- Types of technical reports

HUMANITIES

Ethics in America
- Ethical traditions
- Analysis of issues in relationships
- Tradition versus analysis of issues

Introduction to World Religions
- Dimensions and approaches
- Primal religions, Hinduism, Buddhism, Confucianism, Taoism, Judaism, Christianity, Islam

Principles of Public Speaking
- Topics and purposes
- Organization and supporting materials
- Language, style, and delivery
- Audience analysis and adaptation

PHYSICAL SCIENCE

Astronomy
- The solar system
- The sun and stars
- Our galaxy and the universe
- Measurement

Environment and Humanity: The Race to Save the Planet
- Ecological concepts
- Human impact on the environment
- Environmental management
- Political processes and the future

Here's to Your Health
- Mental health and behavior
- Human development
- Substance use and abuse
- Fitness and nutrition
- Risk factors and disease
- Consumer awareness, environmental concerns

Physical Geology
- Earth materials
- Surface processes
- Internal earth processes
- Applications

Principles of Physical Science I
- Physics: Newton's laws, energy, thermodynamics optics, electricity, and magnetism
- Chemistry: matter, atomic theory and structure, chemical reactions

NOTE:

MOST SCHOOLS DO NOT ACCEPT ALL TESTS FOR ALL PROGRAMS. CHECK WITH THE SCHOOL FROM WHICH YOU EXPECT TO RECEIVE CREDIT.

DANTES

CONTENTS

from the official announcement for instructional purposes

DANTES Subject Standardized Tests (DSSTs)
Receive College Credit for Today's Educational Alternatives

Today, there are many educational alternatives to the classroom—you can learn from your job, your reading, your independent study, and special interests you pursue. You may already have learned the materials covered by some college-level courses.

The DANTES Subject Standardized Tests (DSSTs) is a nationally recognized testing program that gives you the opportunity to receive college credit for learning acquired outside the traditional college classroom. The program, developed by The Chauncey Group International, a subsidiary of Educational Testing Service (ETS), is administered year-round by colleges and universities throughout the United States. Thousands of individuals, particularly adults who are interested in boosting their careers, take the DSSTs annually and receive college credit. MAKE IT A POINT to take advantage of the DSST testing program; it speeds the educational process and provides the flexibility adults need, making earning a degree more feasible.

No prerequisites are required to take the DSSTs; however, because requirements differ from college to college, please check with the school where you are enrolled before taking any DSST. Over 1,200 colleges and universities currently award credit for DSSTs, and the number is growing every day. You can choose from over 35 test titles in the areas of Social Science, Business, Mathematics, Applied Technology, Humanities, and Physical Science. A brief description of each examination is found on pages 6 through 8 of this booklet.

Reach Your Career Goals Through Education

Use DSSTs to help you earn your degree, get a promotion, or simply demonstrate that you have college-level knowledge in subjects relevant to your work.

Save Time...

You don't have to sit through classes when you already know through your experiences most of what is being taught and can learn the rest yourself. You might be able to bypass introductory-level courses in subject areas you already know.

Save Money...

DSSTs save you money because the classes you bypass by earning credit through the credit-by-examination program are classes you won't have to pay for on your way to earning your degree. You can use the money instead to take more advanced courses that can be more challenging and rewarding.

Improve Your Chances for College Admission

Each college has its own admission policies; however, having passing scores for DSSTs on your transcript can provide strong evidence of how well you can perform at the college level.

Gain Confidence Performing at a College Level

Many adults returning to college find that lack of confidence is often the greatest hurdle to overcome. DSSTs can show you how successfully you can compete in the college environment because your performance is compared with the performance of college students.

Make Up for Courses You Might Have Missed

You may be ready to graduate from college and find that you are a few credits short of earning your degree. By using semester breaks, vacation time, or leisure time to study independently, you can prepare to take one or more DSSTs and graduate on time.

If You Cannot Attend Regularly Scheduled Classes...

If your lifestyle or responsibilities prevent you from attending regularly scheduled classes, you can earn your college degree from a college offering an external degree program. This type of program allows you to earn your degree by study and experience outside the traditional classroom. Credit is earned by passing credit-by-examinations such as the DSSTs, portfolio assessment, on-line classes, and other distance learning. To learn more, write or call:

Charter Oak College
66 Cedar Street
Newington, Connecticut 01611
(203) 666-4595

Regents College
7 Columbia Circle
Albany, New York 12203-5159
(518) 464-8500

Thomas Edison State College
101 West State Street
Trenton, New Jersey 08608
(609) 984-1150

Other colleges and universities offer external degree or distance learning programs. For additional information, contact the college you plan to attend or:

Center for Adult Learning and Education Credentials
American Council on Education
1 DuPont Circle
Washington, DC 20036
(202) 939-9475

Where to Take DSSTs

DANTES Subject Standardized Tests (DSSTs) are administered at more than 600 locations nationwide. Each location determines the frequency and scheduling of test administrations.

Your college or one near you may be a DSSTs test site. The free booklet DSST Participating Colleges and Universities lists all DSST test sites and their addresses and phone numbers so you can contact them about scheduling testing. In addition to listing DSST test sites, DSST Participating Colleges and Universities also lists colleges that award DSST credits.

DSST Participating Colleges and Universities is available by writing: DANTES Program, The Chauncey Group International, 664 Rosedale Road, Princeton, New Jersey 08540. You may also order by e-mail at DANTES@Chauncey.com. Please be sure to include your complete name and mailing address.

Earning Credit for DSST Examinations

Credit is awarded for passing scores on DSST exams at more than 1,200 colleges and universities in the United States.

To find out whether or not the college of your choice awards credit for passing DSST scores, contact the admissions office or counseling and testing office. The college can also provide information on the scores required for awarding credit, the number of credit hours awarded, and any courses that can be bypassed with satisfactory scores.

It is important that you contact the college of your choice as early as possible because colleges' credit-awarding policies differ.

Arranging for DSST test administration

After you have selected a college that administers DSSTs, you will need to contact their representative listed in the DSST Participating Colleges and Universities to make arrangements for date and time of testing. Please be aware that certain colleges provide DSST testing services to enrolled students only.

The fee to take a DSST is $27 per test. This fee entitles you to two score reports after the test is scored. One will be sent directly to you and the other will be sent directly to the college or university of your choice. You may pay the fee with a certified check or money order made payable to DANTES Program or you may charge the fee to your Visa, MasterCard, or American Express credit card.

In addition, the test site may also require a test administration fee for each examination, to be paid directly to the institution. Contact the test site to determine its fee and payment policy.

Other Testing Arrangements

If you are unable to find a test site near your location, you may want to contact the testing office of a local accredited college or university to determine whether a representative from that office will agree to administer the test(s) to you on a one-time only basis. The school's representative should then contact the DANTES Client Services Representative at (609) 720-6532 to arrange for this special permission.

If you are a civilian at or near a military base and you do not have access to a civilian test center, you may want to contact the base education officer to see whether security and space permit you to test on the base. This decision is based on the discretion of the base representative.

Testing Accommodations for Students with Disabilities

The Chauncey Group International (Chauncey Group) is committed to serving test takers with disabilities by providing services and reasonable testing accommodations as set forth in the provisions of the Americans with Disabilities Act (ADA). If you have a disability, as prescribed by the ADA, and require special testing services or arrangements, please contact the test administrator at the test site. You will be asked to submit to the test administrator documentation of your disability and your request for special accommodations. The test administrator will then forward your documentation along with your request for testing accommodations to the Chauncey Group for approval. Please submit your request as well in advance of your test date as possible so that we may have the opportunity to make the necessary accommodations.

Only test takers with documented disabilities are eligible for special accommodations.

Description of the DSST Examinations

Mathematics

- **Fundamentals of College Algebra** covers mathematical concepts such as fundamental algebraic operations; linear, absolute value; quadratic equations, inequalities, radials, exponents and logarithms, factoring polynomials and graphing.

- **Principles of Statistics** tests the understanding of the various topics of statistics, both qualitatively and quantitatively, and the ability to apply statistical methods to solve a variety of problems. The topics included in this test are descriptive statistics; correlation and regression; and probability.

Social Science

- **Art of the Western World** deals with the history of art during the following periods: classical; Romanesque and Gothic; early Renaissance; high Renaissance, Baroque; rococo; neoclassicism and romanticism; realism, impressionism and post-impressionism; early twentieth century; and post-World War II.

- **Contemporary Western Europe: 1946 - 1990** tests the knowledge of basic facts and terms and the understanding of concepts and principles related to the areas of the historical background of the aftermath of the Second World War and rebuilding of Europe, national political systems, and issues in Western European societies.

- **An Introduction to the Modern Middle East** emphasizes core knowledge (including geography, Judaism, Christianity, Islam, ethnicity); nineteenth-century European impact; twentieth-century Western influences; World Wars I and II; new nations and Soviet-United States rivalry; the Suez Crisis; the Iranian Revolution; the Soviet invasion of Afghanistan, and the Persian Gulf Crisis.

- **Human/Cultural Geography** includes the Earth and basic facts (coordinate systems, maps, physiography, atmosphere, soils and vegetation, water); culture and environment, spatial processes (social processes, modern economic systems, settlement patterns, political geography); and regional geography.

- **Rise and Fall of the Soviet Union** covers Russia under the Old Regime; the Revolutionary Period; New Economic Policy; Pre-war Stalinism; The Second World War; Post-war Stalinism; The Krushchev Years; The Brezhnev Era; and reform and collapse.

- **A History of the Vietnam War** covers the history of the roots of the Vietnam War; the First Vietnam War (1946-1954); pre-war developments (1954-1963); American involvement in the Vietnam War; Tet (1968); Vietnamizing the War (1968-1973); Cambodia and Laos; peace; legacies and lessons.

- **The Civil War and Reconstruction** covers the Civil War from pre-secession (1861) through Reconstruction. It includes causes of the war; secession; Fort Sumter; the war in the east and in the west; major battles; the political situation; assassination of Lincoln; end of the Confederacy; and Reconstruction.

- **Foundations of Education** includes topics such as contemporary issues in education; past and current influences on education (philosophies, democratic ideals, social/economic influences); and the interrelationships between contemporary issues and influences.

- **Life-span Developmental Psychology** covers models and theories; methods of study; ethical issues; biological development; perception, learning and memory; cognition and language; social, emotional, and personality development; social behaviors, family life cycle, extrafamilial settings; singlehood and cohabitation; occupational development and retirement; adjustment to life stresses; and bereavement and loss.

- **Drug and Alcohol Abuse** includes such topics as drug use in society; classification of drugs; pharmacological principles; alcohol (types, effects of, alcoholism); general principles and use of sedative hypnotics, narcotic analgesics, stimulants, and hallucinogens; other drugs (inhalants, steroids); and prevention/treatment.

- **General Anthropology** deals with anthropology as a discipline; theoretical perspectives; physical anthropology; archaeology; social organization; economic organization; political organization; religion; and modernization and application of anthropology.

- **Introduction to Law Enforcement** includes topics such as history and professional movement of law enforcement; overview of the U.S. criminal justice system; police systems in the U.S.; police organization, management, and issues; and U.S. law and precedents.

- **Criminal Justice** deals with criminal behavior (crime in the U.S., theories of crime, types of crime); the criminal justice system (historical origins, legal foundations, due process); police; the court system (history and organization, adult court system, juvenile court, pre-trial and post-trial processes); and corrections.

- **Fundamentals of Counseling** covers historical development (significant influences and people); counselor roles and functions; the counseling relationship; and theoretical approaches to counseling.

Business

- **Principles of Finance** deals with financial statements and planning; time value of money; working capital management; valuation and characteristics; capital budgeting; cost of capital; risk and return; and international financial management.

- **Principles of Financial Accounting** includes topics such as general concepts and principles, accounting cycle and classification; transaction analysis; accruals and deferrals; cash and internal control; current accounts; long- and short-term liabilities; capital stock; and financial statements.

- **Personnel/Human Resource Management** covers general employment issues; job analysis; training and development; performance appraisals; compensation issues; security issues; personnel legislation and regulation; labor relations and current issues.

- **Organizational Behavior** deals with the study of organizational behavior (scientific approaches, research designs, data collection methods); individual processes and characteristics; interpersonal and group processes and characteristics; organizational processes and characteristics; and change and development processes.

- **Principles of Supervision** deals with the roles and responsibilities of the supervisor; management functions (planning, organization and staffing, directing at the supervisory level); and other topics (legal issues, stress management, union environments, quality concerns).

- **Business Law II** covers topics such as sales of goods; debtor and creditor relations; business organizations; property; and commercial paper.

- **Introduction to Computers with Programming** in Basic includes topics such as history and technological generations; hardware/software; applications to information technology; program development; data management; communications and connectivity; computing and society; and programming in BASIC.

- **Management Information Systems** covers systems theory, analysis and design of systems, hardware and software; database management; telecommunications; management of the MIS functional area and informational support.

- **Introduction to Business** deals with economic issues affecting business; international business; government and business; forms of business ownership; small business, entrepreneurship and franchise; management process; human resource management; production and operations; marketing management; financial management; risk management and insurance; and management and information systems.

- **Money and Banking** covers the role and kinds of money; commercial banks and other financial intermediaries; central banking and the Federal Reserve system; money and macroeconomics activity; monetary policy in the U.S.; and the international monetary system.

- **Personal Finance** includes topics such as financial goals and values; budgeting; credit and debt; major purchases; taxes, insurance, investments, and retirement and estate planning.

- **Business Mathematics** deals with basic operations with integers, fractions, and decimals; round numbers; ratios; averages; business graphs; simple interest; compound interest and annuities; net pay and deductions; discounts and markups; depreciation and net worth; corporate securities; distribution of ownership; and stock and asset turnover.

Physical Science

- **Astronomy** covers the history of astronomy, celestial mechanics; celestial systems; astronomical instruments; the solar system; nature and evolution; the galaxy; the universe; determining astronomical distances; and life in the universe.

- **Here's to Your Health** covers mental health and behavior; human development and relationships; substance abuse; fitness and nutrition; risk factors, disease, and disease prevention; and safety, consumer awareness, and environmental concerns.

- **Environment and Humanity** deals with topics such as ecological concepts (ecosystems, global ecology, food chains and webs); environmental impacts; environmental management and conservation; and political processes and the future.

- **Principles of Physical Science I** includes physics: Newton's Laws of Motion; energy and momentum; thermodynamics; wave and optics; electricity and magnetism; chemistry: properties of matter; atomic theory and structure; and chemical reactions.

- **Physical Geology** covers Earth materials; igneous, sedimentary, and metamorphic rocks; surface processes (weathering, groundwater, glaciers, oceanic systems, deserts and winds, hydrologic cycle); internal Earth processes; and applications (mineral and energy resources, environmental geology).

Applied Technology

- **Technical Writing** covers topics such as theory and practice of technical writing; purpose, content, and organizational patterns of common types of technical documents; elements of various technical reports; and technical editing. Students may write a short essay on one of the technical topics provided. The essay will not be scored by the Chauncey Group; however, a copy of the essay will be provided with the score report or transcript.

Humanities

- **Ethics in America** deals with ethical traditions (Greek views, Biblical traditions, moral law, consequential ethics, feminist ethics); ethical analysis of issues arising in interpersonal and personal-societal relationships and in professional and occupational roles; and relationships between ethical traditions and the ethical analysis of situations. Students may write an essay to analyze a morally problematic situation in terms of issues relevant to a decision and arguments for alternative positions. The essay will not be scored by the The Chauncey Group; however, a copy of the essay will be provided with the score report or transcript.

- **Introduction to World Religions** covers topics such as dimensions and approaches to religion; primal religions; Hinduism; Buddhism; Confucianism; Taoism; Judaism; Christianity; and Islam.

- **Principles of Public Speaking** consists of two parts: Part One requires the student to record an impromptu persuasive speech that will be scored. Part Two consists of multiple-choice questions covering considerations of public speaking; audience analysis; purposes of speeches; structure/organization; content/supporting materials; research; language and style; delivery; communication apprehension; listening and feedback; and criticism and evaluation.

HOW TO ORDER FACT SHEETS/STUDY GUIDES

For each test, there is a Fact Sheet/Study Guide that gives information about the topics that will be covered, books that would be useful for review, the number of questions on the test, and the passing score recommended by the American Council on Education (ACE) for granting credit. It is recommended that students check with the school where they are enrolled about the school's requirements for earning credit. Some schools set higher standards than the ACE minimum recommendation. The Fact Sheet/Study Guides also contain sample test questions to give you an idea of what the test is like. You may order a free copy of the Fact Sheet/Study Guide you need by completing and mailing in the Fact Sheet/Study Guide Order Form on page 11 or sending an e-mail request to DANTES@Chauncey.com. When sending an e-mail request, please include your name and complete mailing address.

ON THE DAY OF THE EXAMINATION

Here are a few tips to help you on the day of your examination:

- Arrive on time as a courtesy to the test administrator. Remember, many test administrators have responsibilities outside the testing office and may have a specific amount of time allotted for your test administration.

- Have your personal photo identification with you. **Anyone who fails to present a photo I.D. will not be tested.**

- Bring several No.2 (soft-lead) pencils with good erasers, a watch, and a black pen if you will be writing an essay.

- Do not bring books or papers.

- Do not bring an alarm watch that beeps, a telephone, or a phone beeper into the testing room.

- The use of non-programmable calculators, slide rules, scratch paper and/or other materials is permitted for some of the tests. Please refer to the section entitled Auxiliary Test Materials on page 15 for specific information.

DANTES SUBJECT STANDARDIZED TESTS SCORING POLICIES

Your DSST examination scores are reported only to you, unless you request that they be sent elsewhere. If you want your scores sent to a college you must grid the correct code number or write the name and address of the school on your answer sheet at the time you take the test.

Receiving Your Score Report

DSST answer sheets are scanned by computer. Allow four weeks after testing to receive your score report.

Do not call before the allotted time for scoring has elapsed—this will not expedite the processing of your scores. Please note that scores will not be reported to students over the telephone because of privacy and security considerations.

Scoring of Public Speaking Speech and Retention of Essays

The speech portion of Public Speaking will be sent to speech raters who are faculty members at accredited colleges that currently teach the course. These raters have received special training to ensure uniformity. Because of this, scores for the Public Speaking examination are normally available in 6 - 8 weeks. If you take the Public Speaking examination and fail, you may retest after 6 months (180 days) on a different speech topic. You must wait 2 years to re-test using the same speech topic.

The essays for Ethics in America and Technical Writing are optional and thus are not scored by raters. The essays are forwarded to the colleges and universities that you designate, along with your score report, for their use in determining the award of credit.

How to Get Transcripts

To request a transcript, use the form located on page 13. There is a $10 fee for each transcript you request.

Availability/Use of Scores

College score requirements for awarding credit vary. Please contact the college or university in which you are enrolled for information on the minimum score it requires to grant credit.

Candidate scores that have been released to colleges may be used for educational research or validity studies by the receiving colleges or by The Chauncey Group International, but the names of individuals will not be revealed or attached to particular scores.

Score Validity

The DANTES Program is obligated to report scores that accurately reflect the performance of the test taker. The program maintains test administration and test security standards designed to assure that all test takers are given the same opportunity to demonstrate their abilities and to prevent any test taker from gaining an unfair advantage.

The DANTES Program reserves the right to cancel any test score if the test taker engages in misconduct, if there is a testing irregularity, or if there is reason to question the score's validity.

Reviews of questionable scores are confidential. If it is necessary to cancel scores that have already been reported, score users are notified, but the reasons for cancellation are not disclosed.

FREQUENTLY ASKED QUESTIONS

How should I study for the examinations?

For each of the DSSTs there is a Fact Sheet/Study Guide which outlines the topics covered by each test. Each Fact Sheet/Study Guide includes a list of sample questions and a list of recommended references for you to use. You may order a free copy of the Fact Sheet/Study Guides you need by completing and mailing the Fact Sheet/Study Guide Order Form on page 11 or by sending an e-mail request to DANTES@chauncey.com. Please include your name and complete mailing address.

In order to pass the test, must I study from one of the recommended references?

The recommended references are a listing of books that were currently being used as text books for the same course title at the time the test was written. If some time has passed since then, you may have difficulty finding the exact title or edition of the book. You might want to consider visiting the bookstore of a local college or university and comparing the text book they currently use for the same class title to the topics listed on the Fact Sheet/Study Guide. If the topics listed on the Fact Sheet/Study Guide are covered by the selected textbook, then you should be reasonably prepared for the test by studying that text book.

Is there a penalty for guessing on the tests?

There is no penalty for guessing on the DANTES Subject Standardized Tests (DSSTs), so you should mark an answer for each question.

How much time will I have to complete the test?

Many DSSTs can be completed within 90 minutes; however, additional time can be allowed if necessary.

What should I do if I find an error in a test question?

If you think there is an error in a test question or any aspect of a test administration, continue with the test, but report the information to the testing supervisor. This may be done after the test by asking that it be noted on the Supervisor's Irregularity Report or by writing to DANTES Program, The Chauncey Group International, Princeton, NJ 08540 and indicating the form and question number(s) or circumstances as well as your name and address.

Will my test scores be released without my permission?

Your test score will not be released to anyone other than the school you designate on your answer sheet unless you write to us and ask us to send a transcript elsewhere. Instructions about how to do this can be found on your score report. Your scores may be used for research purposes, but individual scores are never made public nor are individuals identified if research findings for a group are made public.

If I do not achieve a passing score on the test, how long must I wait until I can take the test again?

If you do not receive a score on the test that will enable you to obtain credit for the course, you may take the test again after six months (180 days). Please do not attempt to take the test before six months (180 days) have passed because you will receive a score report marked invalid and will have wasted the time and the money you invested in retesting. There must be 180 days between test dates in order for your score report to be valid.

Can my test scores be canceled?

The test administrator is required to report any irregularities to the DANTES Program. The consequence of bringing unauthorized materials into the testing room or giving or receiving help will be the forfeiture of your test fee. The DANTES Program reserves the right to cancel scores and not issue score reports in such situations.

What can I do if I feel that my test scores were not accurately reported?

If you have reason to believe that your score(s) were not accurately reported, you may request to have your answer sheet reviewed and hand scored. There is a $10 fee for this service. Please submit a check or money order for $10 payable to DANTES Program with your request in writing for score verification to: DANTES Program, P.O. Box 6604, Princeton, NJ 08541-6604. Include your full name, the test title, the date you took the test, and your Social Security number. We will notify you of the results of hand scoring and, if your scores were not accurate, a corrected score report will be forwarded to you and to any school to which score reports were sent. In the event that a scoring error occurred, your $10 fee will be refunded.

What does ACE recommendation mean?

The ACE recommendation is the minimum passing score recommended by the American Council on Education for any given test. It is equivalent to the average score of students in the DANTES norming sample who received a grade of C for the course. Some schools require a score higher than the ACE recommendation.

How long are my test scores kept on file?

Test scores are kept on file for a period of 20 years.

REMEMBER TO MAKE IT A POINT

You are always learning, whether it be inside a classroom, on your job, or running a household. You can gain experience through retail sales experience, parenting, reading, hobbies (such as Toastmaster's), and non-credit business training. MAKE IT A POINT to get credit for what you already know with DANTES Subject Standardized Tests.

DANTES SUBJECT STANDARDIZED TESTS (DSSTs)

FACT SHEET ❖ ORDER FORM

INSTRUCTIONS:

Please ship the quantities of the DANTES Fact Sheets on the reverse side to:

Name _____

Address _____

City _____ State _____ Zip Code _____

Today's Date _____

To place your order, please mail the completed form to:

The DANTES Program
The Chauncey Group International
PO Box 6604, MS-23P
Princeton, NJ 08541-6604

Fax: (609) 720-6800
For confirmation of receipt of FAX, call: 609-720-6726

For information on The DANTES Program,
call (609) 720-6740.

Fact Sheets for DANTES Subject Standardized Tests

Quantity	Title	Quantity	Title
	MATHEMATICS		**PHYSICAL SCIENCE**
_____	Fundamentals of College Algebra	_____	Astronomy
_____	Principles of Statistics	_____	Here's to Your Health
		_____	Environment and Humanity: The Race to Save the Planet
	SOCIAL SCIENCE	_____	Principles of Physical Science I
_____	Art of the Western World	_____	Physical Geology
_____	Contemporary Western Europe: 1946-1990		
_____	An Introduction to the Modern Middle East		**APPLIED TECHNOLOGY**
_____	Human/Cultural Geography	_____	Technical Writing
_____	Rise and Fall of the Soviet Union		
_____	A History of the Vietnam War		**HUMANITIES**
_____	The Civil War and Reconstruction		
_____	Foundations of Education	_____	Ethics in America
_____	Lifespan Developmental Psychology	_____	Introduction to World Religions
_____	General Anthropology	_____	Principles of Public Speaking
_____	Drug and Alcohol Abuse		
_____	Introduction to Law Enforcement		
_____	Criminal Justice		
_____	Fundamentals of Counseling		
	BUSINESS		
_____	Principles of Finance		
_____	Principles of Financial Accounting		
_____	Personnel/Human Resource Management		
_____	Organizational Behavior		
_____	Principles of Supervision		
_____	Business Law II		
_____	Introduction to Computers with Programming in BASIC		
_____	Introduction to Business		
_____	Money and Banking		
_____	Personal Finance		
_____	Management Information Systems		
_____	Business Mathematics		

DANTES SUBJECT STANDARDIZED TESTS (DSSTs)

CIVILIAN TRANSCRIPT REQUEST FORM FOR DSST SCORES

**TRANSCRIPT REQUEST FORM
FOR DSST SCORES**

To avoid a delay, do not send a letter with this form.

FEE:

A $10 fee is charged for **each** transcript requested. A transcript may include any or all DSST scores.

Enclose a check or money order payable to DANTES Program. If you prefer to pay for your transcript with a credit card, please supply the information below. Your account will be charged with the total amount due. Incomplete forms or forms received without fees will be returned to the requester. **DO NOT SEND CASH OR STAMPS.**

SEND COMPLETED FORM TO:

DANTES Program
The Chauncey Group International
P.O. Box 6604
Princeton, NJ 08541-6604

☐ Check or Money Order enclosed (In U.S. Dollars)   Please charge my   ☐ MasterCard   ☐ Visa   ☐ American Express

My credit card number is: _____   Expiration date: _____ / _____
                                                                    Month   Year

— — — — — - — — — — — - — — — — — - — — — —

PLEASE PRINT ALL INFORMATION REQUESTED BELOW.

_____ / _____
Last Name (Include Maiden Name or Former Last Names)   First   MI   Social Security Number

_____ / _____
Present Address   Number and Street   Date of Birth

_____   _____
City and State   Zip Code   Phone Number

I understand that my signature permits DANTES to release my
transcript to the designated recipient(s).

_____
(Signature)

Please prepare my transcript and include the following (check only one):

☐ Scores on all tests below

☐ Only test scores that are at or above
   the ACE Recommended Minimum Score

☐ Only scores on tests named

TEST TITLES: _____

_____

Approximate Date of Last DANTES Test _____

☐ Please send a copy of my transcript to the following school(s) (**$10.00 per transcript**):

School Name	School Name
Attn:	Attn:
Address	Address
City & State Zip Code	City & State Zip Code

13

Notes for Test Takers

Here is some information about the DANTES test you are planning to take that you may find helpful.

Preparing for the Test

For each test, there is a fact sheet that gives information about the topics that will be covered, books that would be useful for review, the number of questions on the test, and the minimum score recommended by the American Council on Education (ACE) for credit. (You should check the passing score with your school; some have set higher standards than the ACE minimum recommendation.) Some of the fact sheets also contain sample test questions to give you an idea of what the test is like. Copies of these sheets are available without charge from the test administrator, your counselor, by phone at 609-720-6740 or by e-mail at DANTES@chauncey.com.

Guessing

There is no penalty for guessing on the DANTES Subject Standardized Tests, so you should mark an answer for each question.

Test Timing

These tests are untimed. It generally takes about 11/2 hours to take a DANTES Subject Standardized Test; however, you may work longer if necessary.

Test Materials

The use of non-programmable calculators, slide rules, scratch paper and/or other materials is permitted for some of the tests. The test administrator has information about whether the test(s) you are planning to take fall into this category and which materials are permitted. If you wish to bring any materials into the test room, please check before testing to be sure they are permitted.

Subject Standardized Tests

Test Administration

If you think there is an error in a test question, continue with the test, but report the information to The Chauncey Group International. This may be done by telling the supervisor after the test, asking that it be noted on the Supervisor's Irregularity Report, by writing to **The Chauncey Group, DANTES Program, CN-6604, Princeton, NJ 08541-6604**, indicating the form and question numbers as well as your name and address.

Confidentiality

Your test score on your test will not be released to anyone other than the school you designate on your answer sheet unless you write to us and ask us to send a transcript elsewhere. Instructions about how to do this will be found on your score report. Your scores may be used for research purposes, but individual scores are never made public nor are individuals identified if research findings for a group are made public.

Students with Disabilities

Special testing arrangements are authorized for students with disabilities. If you are in need of this service, speak to your test administrator in advance of the testing. A reader or writer may be used or other special arrangements may be made to minimize the effect of your disability on your score.

Retesting

If you do not receive a score on the test that will enable you to obtain credit for the course, you may take the test again after six months (180 days). Please do not attempt to retake the test before six months (180 days) have elapsed because you will receive a score report marked invalid and will have wasted the time and money you invested in retesting.

Score Cancellation

The test administrator is required to report any irregularities to The Chauncey Group. The consequences of bringing unauthorized materials into the testing room or giving or receiving help will be the forfeiture of your test fee. The Chauncey Group reserves the right to cancel scores and not issue score reports in such situations.

Score Verification

If you have reason to believe that your score(s) were not accurately reported, you may request to have your answer sheet hand scored. There is a $10 fee for this service. Please submit a check or money order for $10 payable to **DANTES Program** with your request in writing for score verification to: **The Chauncey Group International, P.O. Box 6604, Princeton, NJ 08541-6604**. Include your full name, the test title, the date you took the test and your Social Security number. We will notify you of the results of hand scoring and, if your scores were not accurate, a corrected score report will be forwarded to you and any school, to which score reports were sent. In the event that a Chauncey Group error occurred, your money will be refunded.

DANTES
Subject Standardized Tests

ACE Credit
Recommendations

American Council on Education
Credit Recommendations

Test Form Number	Title	Credit Amount in Semester Hours	Minimum Score
MATHEMATICS			
SF/SG 424	Fundamentals of College Algebra	3B	47
SE 450	Principles of Statistics	3B	48
SOCIAL SCIENCE			
SE 461	Art of the Western World	3B	48
SE 465	Contemporary Western Europe: 1946-1990	3B	48
SE 469	An Introduction to the Modern Middle East	3B	44
SF/SG 470	Human/Cultural Geography	3B	48
SE 471	Rise and Fall of the Soviet Union	3BU	45
SF 473	A History of the Vietnam War	3B	49
SE/SF 483	The Civil War and Reconstruction	3BU	47
SE 489	Foundations of Education	3B	46
SF/SG 490	Lifespan Developmental Psychology	3B	46
SF 494	General Anthropology	3B	47
SE 495	Drug and Alcohol Abuse	3BU	49
SG/SH 497	Introduction to Law Enforcement	3B	45
SF/SG 498	Criminal Justice	3B	49
SG/SH 562	Fundamentals of Counseling	3B	45
BUSINESS			
SF/SG 524	Principles of Finance	3BU	46
SF 525	Principles of Financial Accounting	3B	49
SF 530	Personnel/Human Resource Management	3B	48
SF/SG 531	Organizational Behavior	3B	48
SE/SF 532	Principles of Supervision	3B	46
SE 534	Business Law II	3BU	52
SG/SH 536	Introduction to Computing	3B	45
SE/SF 543	Introduction to Business	3B	46
SG/SH 548	Money and Banking	3BU	48
SE 550	Personal Finance	3B	46
SE 551	Management Information Systems	3BU	46
SF/SG 812	Business Mathematics	3B	48

Unlimited reproduction of this sheet is allowed.

Test Form Number	Title	Credit Amount in Semester Hours	Minimum Score
PHYSICAL SCIENCE			
SF 500	Astronomy	3B	48
SF/SG 508	Here's to Your Health	3B	48
SF/SG 511	Environment and Humanity: The Race to Save the Planet	3B	46
SE 512	Principles of Physical Science I	3B	47
SF 519	Physical Geology	3B	46
APPLIED TECHNOLOGY			
SF/SG 820	Technical Writing (*TWE Technical Writing Essay*)	3B	46
HUMANITIES			
SF/SG 474	Ethics in America (*SF 474 Ethics in America Essay*)	3B	46
SE 496	Introduction to World Religions	3B	49
SE/SF 815*	Principles of Public Speaking	3B	47

In addition to a minimum score of 47 on the multiple-choice test, an examinee must also receive a passing grade on the speech.

B = Baccalaureate Program
BU = Baccalaureate Upper Division

dsst

DANTES Subject Standardized Tests

Fact Sheet

PRINCIPLES OF FINANCE

TEST INFORMATION

This test was developed to enable schools to award credit to students for knowledge equivalent to that which is learned by students taking the course. The school may choose to award college credit to the student based on the achievement of a passing score. The passing score for each examination is determined by the school based on recommendations from the American Council on Education (ACE). This minimum credit-awarding score is equal to the mean score of students in the norming sample who received a grade of C in the course. Some schools set their own standards for awarding credit and may require a higher score than the ACE recommendation. Students should obtain this information from the institution where they expect to receive credit.

The use of non-programmable calculators is permitted during the test. Scratch paper for computations should be provided.

CONTENT

The following topics, which are commonly taught in courses on this subject, are covered by this examination.

		Approximate Percent
I.	Financial Statements and Planning A. Ratio analysis B. Break-even C. Leverage	**25%**
II.	Time Value of Money A. Present value B. Future value	**15%**
III.	Working Capital Management A. Short-term sources of funds B. Management of short-term assets	**18%**
IV.	Valuation and Characteristics of Stocks and Bonds A. Long-term debt B. Common stock	**11%**
V.	Capital Budgeting	**13%**
VI.	Cost of Capital	**11%**
VII.	Risk and Return	**4%**
VIII.	International Financial Management	**3%**

Questions on the test require candidates to demonstrate the following abilities. Some questions may require more than one of these abilities.

- Knowledge of basic facts and terms (about 35 to 40 % of the examination)

- Understanding of the concepts and principles (about 50 % of the examination)

- Ability to apply knowledge to specific problems and situations (about 10 to 15% of the examination)

SAMPLE QUESTIONS

Note: If a question requires data from time-value tables, these tables will be provided in the test book.

1. Which of the following statements is true about a stock split?

   (A) It increases equity.
   (B) It decreases assets.
   (C) It increases retained earnings.
   (D) It decreases the par value of the stock.

from the official announcement for instructional purposes

 *A subsidiary of* Educational Testing Service

2. When a firm pays a cash dividend, the firm's balance sheet is affected in which of the following ways?

(A) Assets and equity remain the same.
(B) Assets decrease and equity increases.
(C) Assets and liabilities decrease.
(D) Assets and equity decrease.

3. The degree of financial leverage measures the responsiveness of

(A) earnings to changes in operating expenses
(B) earnings to changes in output
(C) earnings before taxes to changes in operating income
(D) operating income to changes in net income

4. In linear break-even analysis, a decrease in fixed costs, if other factors remain constant, will cause the break-even point and the degree of operating leverage to do which of the following?

	Break-even Point	Degree of Operating Leverage
(A)	Increase	Decrease
(B)	Decrease	Decrease
(C)	Decrease	Increase
(D)	Increase	Increase

5. Which of the following terms of trade credit is most favorable for the buyer?

(A) 2/15 net 30
(B) 2/15 net 45
(C) 3/10 net 30
(D) 3/15 net 45

6. The internal rate of return for a project will be higher if the

(A) cost of capital is lower
(B) cost of capital is higher
(C) initial investment is lower
(D) initial investment is higher

7. If the internal rate of return of two mutually exclusive investments is less than the firm's cost of capital, the firm should make which of the following investments, if any?

(A) The shorter term investment
(B) The investment with the lower internal rate of return
(C) The investment with the higher internal rate of return
(D) None of the above

8. Which of the following is associated with a stock dividend as opposed to a cash dividend?

(A) An increase in assets
(B) An increase in equity
(C) A decrease in assets
(D) No change in liabilities

9. The primary responsibility of a financial manager is to maximize the firm's

(A) stockholder wealth
(B) sales
(C) earnings
(D) profits

10. Which two of the following would be preferable to bond owners?

I.   A debt ratio of 50% rather than 20%
II. A debt ratio of 20% rather than 50%
III. A times-interest-earned of 2.0 rather than 5.0
IV. A times-interest-earned 5.0 rather than 2.0

(A) I and III
(B) I and IV
(C) II and III
(D) II and IV

11. Which of the following will cause a currency outflow from the United States?

(A) The purchase of United States plants and equipment by Japanese investors
(B) The maintenance of United States military bases in Europe
(C) The trading of Japanese yen for United States dollars by Japanese investors
(D) The return of income from United States investments in Europe

STUDYING FOR THE EXAMINATION

The following is a list of reference publications that were being used as textbooks in college courses of the same or similar title at the time the test was developed. Appropriate textbooks for study are not limited to those listed below. If you wish to obtain study resources to prepare for the examination, you may reference either the current edition of the following titles or textbooks currently used at a local college or university for the same class title. It is recommended that you reference **more than one textbook** on the topics outlined in this fact sheet. You should **begin by checking textbook content against the content outline** included on the front page of this Fact Sheet **before** selecting textbooks that cover the test content from which to study. Textbooks may be found at the campus bookstore of a local college or university offering a course on the subject.

Sources for study material suggested but not limited to the following:

Block, Stanley B. and Geoffrey A. Hirt. *Foundations of Financial Management*. Chicago, IL: Irwin, current edition.

Dickerson, Bodil, B.J. Campsey, and Eugene F. Brigham. *Introduction to Financial Management*. Fort Worth, TX: Dryden Press, current edition.

Gitman, Lawrence J. *Foundations of Managerial Finance*. New York: Harper Collins, current edition.

Kolb, Burton A. and Richard F. DeMong. *Principles of Financial Management*. Plano, TX: Business Publications, current edition.

Mayo, Herbert B. *Finance: An Introduction*. Fort Worth, TX: Dryden Press, current edition.

Melicher, Ronald W., Edgar A. Norton and Merle T. Welshans. *Finance: Introduction to Markets,* *Institutions and Management*. Cincinnati, OH: South-Western Publishing Co., current edition.

Roden, Payton Foster and George A. Christy. *Finance: Environment and Decisions*. New York: Harper & Row, current edition.

Current textbook used by a local college or university for a course on the subject.

CREDIT RECOMMENDATIONS

The Center For Adult Learning and Educational Credentials of the American Council on Education (ACE) has reviewed and evaluated the DSST examination development process. The American Council on Education has made the following recommendations:

Area or Course Equivalent:	Principles of Finance
Level:	Upper-level Baccalaureate
Amount of Credit:	Three (3) semester hours
Source:	ACE Commission on Educational Credit and Credentials

INFORMATION

Colleges and universities that would like additional information about the national norming, or assistance in local norming or score validation studies should write to: DSST Program, Mail Stop 11-P, The Chauncey Group International, 664 Rosedale Road, Princeton, New Jersey 08540.

It is advisable that schools develop a consistent policy about awarding credit based on scores from this test and that the policy be reviewed periodically. The Chauncey Group will be happy to help schools in this effort.

HOW TO TAKE A TEST

You have studied hard, long, and conscientiously.

With your official admission card in hand, and your heart pounding, you have been admitted to the examination room.

You note that there are several hundred other applicants in the examination room waiting to take the same test.

They all appear to be equally well prepared.

You know that nothing but your best effort will suffice. The "moment of truth" is at hand: you now have to demonstrate objectively, in writing, your knowledge of content and your understanding of subject matter.

You are fighting the most important battle of your life — to pass and/or score high on an examination which will determine your career and provide the economic basis for your livelihood.

What extra, special things should you know and should you do in taking the examination?

BEFORE THE TEST

YOUR PHYSICAL CONDITION IS IMPORTANT

If you are not well, you can't do your best work on tests. If you are half asleep, you can't do your best either. Here are some tips:

1. Get about the same amount of sleep you usually get. Don't stay up all night before the test, either partying or worrying — DON'T DO IT.

2. If you wear glasses, be sure to wear them when you go to take the test. This goes for hearing aids, too.

3. If you have any physical problems that may keep you from doing your best, be sure to tell the person giving the test. If you are sick or in poor health, you really cannot do your best on any test. You can always come back and take the test some other time.

AT THE TEST

EXAMINATION TECHNIQUES

1. Read the *general* instructions carefully. These are usually printed on the first page of the examination booklet. As a rule, these instructions refer to the timing of the examination; the fact that you should not start work until the signal and must stop work at a signal, etc. If there are any *special* instructions, such as a choice of questions to be answered, make sure that you note this instruction carefully.

2. **When you are ready to start work on the examination, that is as soon as the signal has been given, read the instructions to each question booklet, underline any key words or phrases, such as** *least, best, outline, describe,* **and the like.** In this way you will tend to answer as requested rather than discover on reviewing your paper that you *listed without describing,* that you selected the *worst* choice rather than the *best* choice, etc.

3. If the examination is of the objective or so-called multiple-choice type, that is, each question will also give a series of possible answers: A, B, C, or D, and you are called upon to select the best answer and write the letter next to that answer on your answer paper, it is advisable to start answering each question in turn. There may be anywhere from 50 to 100 such questions in the three or four hours allotted and you can see how much time would be taken if you read through all the questions before beginning to answer any. Furthermore, if you come across a question or a group of questions which you know would be difficult to answer, it would undoubtedly affect your handling of all the other questions.

4. If the examination is of the essay-type and contains but a few questions, it is a moot point as to whether you should read all the questions before starting to answer any one. Of course if you are given a choice, say five out of seven and the like, then it is essential to read all the questions so you can eliminate the two which are most difficult. If, however, you are asked to answer all the questions, there may be danger in trying to answer the easiest one first because you may find that you will spend too much time on it. The best technique is to answer the first question, then proceed to the second, etc.

5. Time your answers. Before the examination begins, write down the time it started, then add the time allowed for the examination and write down the time it must be completed, then divide the time available somewhat as follows:

   a. If 3 ½ hours are allowed, that would be 210 minutes. If you have 80 objective-type questions, that would be an average of about 2 ½ minutes per question. Allow yourself no more than 2 minutes per question, or a total of 160 minutes, which will permit about 50 minutes to review.

   b. If for the time allotment of 210 minutes, there are 7 essay questions to answer, that would average about 30 minutes a question. Give yourself only 25 minutes per question so that you have about 35 minutes to review.

6. The most important instruction is *to read each question* and make sure you know what is wanted. The second most important instruction is to *time yourself properly* so that you answer every question. The third most important instruction is to *answer every question*. Guess if you have to but include something for each question, Remember that you will receive no credit for a blank and will probably receive some credit if you write something in answer to an essay question. If you guess a letter, say "B" for a multiple-choice question, you may have guessed right. If you leave a blank as the answer to a multiple-choice question, the examiners may respect your feelings but it will not add a point to your score. Some exams may penalize you for wrong answers, so in such cases *only*, you may not want to guess unless you have some basis for your answer.

7. Suggestions

   a. Objective-Type Questions

      (1) Examine the question booklet for proper sequence of pages and questions.

      (2) Read all instructions carefully.

      (3) Skip any question which seems too difficult; return to it after all other questions have been answered.

      (4) Apportion your time properly; do not spend too much time on any single question or group of questions.

      (5) Note and underline key words — *all, most, fewest, least, best, worst, same, opposite.*

      (6) Pay particular attention to negatives.

      (7) Note unusual option, e.g., unduly long, short, complex, different or similar in content to the body of the question.

      (8) Observe the use of "hedging" words — *probably, may, most likely, etc.*

      (9) Make sure that your answer is put next to the same number as the question.

      (10) Do not second guess unless you have good reason to believe the second answer is definitely more correct.

      (11) Cross out original answer if you decide another answer is more accurate; do not erase, *until* you are ready to hand your paper in.

      (12) Answer all questions; guess unless instructed otherwise.

      (13) Leave time for review.

b. Essay-Type Questions

    (1) Read each question carefully.

    (2) Determine exactly what is wanted. Underline key words or phrases.

    (3) Decide on outline or paragraph answer.

    (4) Include many different points and elements unless asked to develop any one or two points or elements.

    (5) Show impartiality by giving pros and cons unless directed to select one side only.

    (6) Make and write down any assumptions you find necessary to answer the question.

    (7) Watch your English, grammar, punctuation, choice of words.

    (8) Time your answers; don't crowd material.

8. Answering the Essay Question

Most essay questions can be answered by framing the specific response around several key words or ideas. Here are a few such key words or ideas:

M's: manpower, materials, methods, money, management

P's: purpose, program, policy, plan, procedure, practice, problems, pitfalls, personnel, public relations

a. Six basic steps in handling problems:

    (1) preliminary plan and background development

    (2) collect information, data and facts

    (3) analyze and interpret information, data and facts

    (4) analyze and develop solutions as well as make recommendations

    (5) prepare report and sell recommendations

    (6) install recommendations and follow up effectiveness

b. Pitfalls to Avoid

    (1) *Taking Things for Granted*
    A statement of the situation does not necessarily imply that each of the elements is necessarily true; for example, a complaint may be invalid and biased so that all that can be taken for granted is that a complaint has been registered

    (2) *Considering only one side of a situation*
    Wherever possible, indicate several alternatives and then point out the reasons you selected the best one.

    (3) *Failing to indicate follow up*
    Whenever your answer indicates action on your part, make certain that you will take proper follow-up action to see how successful your recommendations, procedures, or actions turn out to be.

    (4) *Taking too long in answering any single question*
    Remember to time your answers properly.

EXAMINATION SECTION

EXAMINATION SECTION
TEST 1

DIRECTIONS: Each question or incomplete statement is followed by several suggested answers or completions. Select the one that BEST answers the question or completes the statement. *PRINT THE LETTER OF THE CORRECT ANSWER IN THE SPACE AT THE RIGHT.*

1. A company holds a ten-year maturity bond with a stated interest rate of 12%. If investors require a 10% yield on bonds of similar quality, the value of the bond in the coming month will
   A. decrease
   B. increase
   C. remain unchanged
   D. float along with the prime rate

1.____

2. Each of the following is considered to be a MAJOR financial management function EXCEPT
   A. raising funds
   B. financial planning and analysis
   C. managing the accounting system
   D. asset management

2.____

3. When used as a capital budgeting tool, the profitability index of a proposed investment project is determined by
   A. adding the present value of the investment and the cash outflow created by the cost of the investment
   B. dividing the cash outflow created by the cost of the investment by the investment's present value
   C. dividing the present value of the investment by the net present value
   D. dividing the present value of the investment by the cash outflow created by the cost of the investment

3.____

4. In what type of business do all owners have unlimited liability for the firm's debts?
   A. Proprietorship   B. Partnership
   C. Corporation   D. Limited partnership

4.____

5. For manufacturing firms, current assets have historically accounted for about _____% or more of total assets.
   A. 25   B. 40   C. 65   D. 80

5.____

6. Each of the following is a factor involved in the return-on-owners' equity model EXCEPT
   A. profit margin
   B. weighted average cost of capital
   C. equity multiplier
   D. asset turnover

6.____

7. What type of preferred stock gives a corporation the
   right to retire the preferred stock at its option?   7.__
      A. Noncumulative   B. Cumulative
      C. Convertible   D. Callable

8. The principle of hedging generally requires matching   8.__
      A. dollar amounts of current assets with fixed assets
      B. fixed assets with sales volume
      C. the average maturities of assets with liabilities
          and equity
      D. short-term financing with fixed assets

9. Which of the following is generally considered to be good   9.__
   practice in managing a company's investment portfolio?
      A. Considering securities with positive correlations to
          each other
      B. Investing primarily in creditor claims
      C. Adjusting upward to the extent to which an investment
          account can be realized in the case of market decline
      D. Staggering the maturity rates of securities

10. An ordinary annuity is one in which   10.__
       A. the interest rate is fixed for a specified period of
           time
       B. cash flows occur at the beginning of each time
           period
       C. cash flows occur over a period of several years
       D. cash flow amounts occur at the end of each period
           starting with the first cash flow at the end of the
           first year

11. A business's demand for the cash needed to carry out   11.__
    daily operations is referred to as its
       A. transactions motive   B. net working capital
       C. precautionary motive   D. current ratio

12. Which of the following forms of claim in foreign exchange   12.__
    is generally LEAST expensive?
       A. Bill of exchange   B. Time draft
       C. Cable order   D. Sight draft

13. Which of the following financial statements is best for   13.__
    capturing a *snapshot* of a company's overall status at a
    particular point in time?
       A. Cash flow statement   B. Income statement
       C. Trend analysis   D. Balance sheet

14. A financial manager should try to minimize the investment   14.__
    in current assets because of
       A. the need for acceptable credit terms
       B. the cost of financing them
       C. liquidity purposes
       D. the risk involved in holding them

15. The financing provided by accounts payable is estimated   15.___
by means of
   A. multiplying accounts payable by the average inventory
      turnover
   B. subtracting accounts receivable from accounts payable
   C. dividing the cost of goods sold by the average
      inventory turnover
   D. dividing accounts payable by the cost of goods sold

16. Under current tax law, businesses are allowed to depre-   16.___
ciate ____% of their fixed assets in the five-year
property class during the first year.
   A. 6   B. 12   C. 20   D. 32

17. What is the term for the funds remaining after subtract-   17.___
ing current liabilities from current assets?
   A. Net working capital   B. Gross revenue
   C. Retained earnings   D. Financial leverage

18. The management of receivables involves each of the   18.___
following EXCEPT
   A. conducting credit analysis
   B. determining transactions motives
   C. setting credit terms
   D. carrying out collection efforts

Questions 19-20.

DIRECTIONS: Questions 19 and 20 refer to the information below.

Keller Manufacturing is a corporation with 50,000 shares of
common stock outstanding. Its stock is currently traded at $40
per share. Its net sales total $1.4 million and its net income
is $100,000.

19. What is the firm's earnings per share (EPS)?   19.___
   A. $1.00   B. $2.00   C. $2.50   D. $3.25

20. Keller's price-earnings (P/E) ratio is   20.___
   A. 2   B. 5   C. 10   D. 12

21. A loan on which the borrower agrees to make regular   21.___
payments on principal as well as on interest is described
as
   A. compounding   B. combined
   C. balanced   D. amortized

22. Most bonds pay interest   22.___
   A. quarterly   B. semiannually
   C. annually   D. biannually

23. The principal *current* assets of a business typically   23.__
    include each of the following EXCEPT
    A. inventories
    B. prepaid expenses
    C. accounts receivable
    D. cash and marketable securities

24. Which of the following is the most widely used source of   24.__
    short-term funds for businesses?
    A. Commercial paper
    B. Commercial finance companies
    C. Trade credits
    D. Commercial banks

25. Which of the following is typically used as a last resort   25.__
    for the financing of current assets?
    A. Accounts payable
    B. Marketable securities
    C. Accrued liabilities
    D. Short-term bank loans or long-term funds

————

KEY (CORRECT ANSWERS)

1.	B	11.	A
2.	C	12.	B
3.	D	13.	D
4.	B	14.	B
5.	B	15.	C
6.	B	16.	C
7.	D	17.	A
8.	C	18.	B
9.	D	19.	B
10.	D	20.	C

21. D
22. B
23. B
24. D
25. D

————

TEST 2

DIRECTIONS: Each question or incomplete statement is followed by several suggested answers or completions. Select the one that BEST answers the question or completes the statement. *PRINT THE LETTER OF THE CORRECT ANSWER IN THE SPACE AT THE RIGHT.*

1. A limitation associated with the payback period method of capital budgeting is that it   1.____
   A. ignores all cash flows beyond the payback period
   B. does not include a specific estimate of an investment's initial outlay
   C. does not determine the time it will take to recover the initial investment
   D. does not presume the future benefits of an investment

2. Which of the following types of ratios is commonly used to determine a business's net working capital?   2.____
   I. Financial leverage ratio
   II. Acid-test ratio
   III. Asset utilization ratio
   IV. Current ratio

   The CORRECT answer is:
   A. I, II   B. II, IV   C. I, II, III   D. I, III, IV

3. When a financial manager compares potential investment projects during the capital budgeting process, he or she is really comparing   3.____
   A. variance   B. net present values
   C. costs of investment   D. cash flows

4. Typically, the FIRST step in the financial planning process is to   4.____
   A. determine debt-equity fund mix
   B. forecast sales
   C. determine a liquidity ratio
   D. determine profitability

5. In general, which of the following investments involves the greatest risk of default?   5.____
   A. U.S. government bonds   B. Common stocks
   C. Municipal bonds   D. Corporate bonds

6. In which of the following situations would one most likely encounter a present-value annuity-due problem?   6.____
   A. Home mortgages   B. Facility rentals
   C. Leasing arrangements   D. Callable bonds

7. When a company's financial leverage is determined by 7.__
using an equity multiplier ratio, it is calculated by
   A. multiplying total liabilities by owners' equity
   B. dividing total liabilities by total assets
   C. dividing owners' equity by total liabilities
   D. dividing the total assets by owners' equity

8. In the capital budgeting process, the *selection* stage 8.__
typically involves
   A. applying the appropriate capital budgeting techniques
      to help make a final accept or reject decision
   B. reviewing past decisions
   C. discussing the pros and cons of each project
   D. finding potential capital investment opportunities
      and identifying whether a project involves a replace-
      ment decision and/or revenue expansion

9. The link between financial planning and the management of 9.__
working capital, including both current assets and current
liabilities, can be described in terms of a business's
   A. short-term operating cycle
   B. retained earnings
   C. asset turnover ratio
   D. net working capital

10. _____ motives are NOT motives for which business firms 10.__
hold cash and marketable securities.
   A. Precautionary   B. Goodwill
   C. Speculative   D. Transactions

11. In a typical income statement, the starting point 11.__
reflects
   A. current liabilities   B. current assets
   C. variable costs   D. revenues or sales

12. Which of the following stock market indicators demon- 12.__
strates the health and trend of the market?
   A. Trading volume   B. Odd-lot trading
   C. Charts   D. Market breadth

13. What is the term for the process by which savings are 13.__
accumulated in financial institutions and, in turn, lent
or invested by them?
   A. Intermediation   B. Transition
   C. Interplay   D. Transubstantiation

Questions 14-15.

DIRECTIONS: Questions 14 and 15 refer to the information below.

The Longbow Company is evaluating a project for possible
inclusion in its capital budget. The project will require an
$80,000 investment. After-tax cash inflows are estimated at
$24,000 a year for the next four years.

14. What is the approximate payback period for the investment? 14.___
    _____ years.
    A. 1.2   B. 2.7   C. 3.3   D. 4.4

15. Calculate the net present value of the project based on a 15.___
    10% cost of capital (PVIFA = 3.170).
    A. -$3,920   B. -$1,960   C. $7,840   D. $76,080

16. A finance computation involving cash flows that occur at 16.___
    the beginning of each time period is known as a(n) _____
    problem.
    A. discounting   B. annuity due
    C. compounding   D. regular annuity

17. In general, the most critical element in the risk-return 17.___
    analysis of potential investment projects is the correct
    estimation of
    A. the amounts and probability of cash flows
    B. interest rates
    C. resources available for investment
    D. total costs

18. When information is taken from both the income statement 18.___
    and the balance sheet to show how the firm obtained funds
    during the accounting period and how those funds were used,
    this information is typically used to compose a(n)
    A. statement of cash flows
    B. time series analysis
    C. cash transactions statement
    D. asset utilization ratio

19. Which of the following is NOT a section that is included 19.___
    in a Dun & Bradstreet business credit report?
    A. History   B. Character assessment
    C. Operation and location   D. Trade payments

20. Amounts which are owed but not yet paid for are referred 20.___
    to as
    A. real liabilities   B. accrued liabilities
    C. current liabilities D. amortized loans

21. A business firm's cost of common equity capital is   21.___
    considered to be the same as the
    A. weighted average cost of capital on all its invest-
       ments
    B. internal rate of return on its long-term investments
    C. rate of return on long-term debt financing
    D. rate of return expected by investors in the firm's
       common stock

22. Each of the following is considered to be an internal   22.___
    business risk EXCEPT
    A. the death of a key employee
    B. theft
    C. bond market failure
    D. natural disasters

23. For most firms, retained earnings must first be used for   23.__
    A. paying out dividends
    B. paying taxes
    C. repaying business loans
    D. purchasing equipment

24. A company's break-even point for the sale of a particular   24.__
product is revealed through the process of
    A. time series analysis   B. sales forecasting
    C. comparative analysis   D. cost-volume analysis

25. When using the internal rate of return method for capital   25.__
budgeting, the present value interest factor (PVIFA) for
an investment is found by
    A. dividing the initial outlay by the annual cash inflow
        of the investment
    B. dividing the cash inflow annuity amount (annual
        receipt) by the initial outlay
    C. dividing the initial outlay by the cash inflow
        annuity amount
    D. subtracting the initial outlay from the cash inflow
        annuity amount

KEY (CORRECT ANSWERS)

1. A		11. D	
2. B		12. A	
3. B		13. A	
4. B		14. C	
5. B		15. A	
6. C		16. B	
7. D		17. A	
8. A		18. A	
9. A		19. B	
10. B		20. B	

21. D
22. C
23. A
24. D
25. C

TEST 3

DIRECTIONS: Each question or incomplete statement is followed by several suggested answers or completions. Select the one that BEST answers the question or completes the statement. *PRINT THE LETTER OF THE CORRECT ANSWER IN THE SPACE AT THE RIGHT.*

1. Solving for the future value of an amount deposited now will involve each of the following factors EXCEPT
   A. 1 divided by 1 plus the interest rate
   B. the number of periods to compound over
   C. 1 plus the interest rate
   D. present value amount

   1.___

2. Which of the following is NOT a disadvantage associated with being a common stockholder?
   A. When profits are low, other claims may completely absorb available funds
   B. Relatively little control over the firm's activities
   C. Less stability with respect to dividends
   D. Low priority during business liquidation

   2.___

3. The purpose of a liquidity ratio is to
   A. show the ability of a business to meet its short-term obligations
   B. show how well the company uses its assets to support or generate sales
   C. indicate the extent to which assets are financed by borrowed funds and other liabilities
   D. compare profits with sales

   3.___

4. An optimal capital structure
   A. makes maximum use of long-term debt
   B. minimizes the cost of debt and equity funds
   C. relies primarily on short-term funds
   D. stabilizes the value of the firm

   4.___

5. A bank offers an 8% interest rate on its accounts which will compound semiannually. If $1,000 is invested for a period of ten years, what will be the future value of the investment?
   A. $1,763   B. $2,159   C. $2,191   D. $2,222

   5.___

6. Which of the following is a selection technique used to evaluate long-term investment proposals?
   A. Capital budgeting
   B. Working capital management
   C. Sensitivity analysis
   D. Discounting analysis

   6.___

7. Each of the following is a factor involved in calculating   7.__
the future value of an investment EXCEPT the
    A. interest rate
    B. number of periods in years
    C. difference between compounding and discounting rates
    D. present value

8. In risk-return analysis, the dispersion of cash flows is   8.__
denoted by the term
    A. variance   B. net present value
    C. standard deviation   D. expected value

Questions 9-10.

DIRECTIONS: Questions 9 and 10 refer to the information below.

In the previous year, the Earl Company earned $100,000 in net income on net sales of $1.4 million. The company's balance sheet shows that accounts payable plus accrued liabilities were about 15% of sales. Net sales are expected to rise by 10% next year, and the profit margin is expected to hold.

9. Assuming that management at the Earl Company plans to pay   9.__
out about half the company's profits to the owners of the
company, how much internally generated financing would be
available to support Earl's assets?
    A. $45,000   B. $55,000   C. $70,000   D. $110,000

10. How much of Earl's assets would have to be financed with   10.__
external funds?
    A. $45,000   B. $55,000   C. $70,000   D. $110,000

11. Which of the following is NOT typically a capital-budget-   11.__
ing decision?
    A. Ranking projects in terms of their expected returns
    B. Whether to expand existing product lines
    C. Whether to conduct credit analysis of a potential
       purchaser
    D. Whether to replace existing equipment with new
       equipment

12. What is the term for an option to buy a security at a   12.__
specified price during a specified period of time?
    A. Bank acceptance   B. Futures contract
    C. Leverage contract   D. Call contract

13. Which of the following are indirect equity claims?   13.__
    A. Mutual funds   B. Money market funds
    C. Commercial paper   D. Bonds

14. Which of the following will be indicated by estimating   14.__
the time it takes to complete a business's short-term
operating cycle relative to the level of operations?

    I. The extent to which financing will take place through
      accounts payable
   II. The influence of asset turnover on inventories
  III. The size of the investment in accounts receivable
      and inventories

The CORRECT answer is:
  A. I *only*   B. II *only*   C. I, III   D. II, III

15. What is the term for a company's need for funds to take   15.___
    advantage of unexpected price bargains or discounts?
    A. Incidental capital   B. Suppositional assets
    C. Speculative motive   D. Hedge

16. A company's asset turnover component is expressed as   16.___
    A. net income divided by net sales
    B. net sales divided by total assets
    C. total assets divided by net income
    D. net income divided by total assets

17. A financial manager must set a rate of return that the   17.___
    company needs to earn on its asset investments in order
    to cover the cost of debt and still leave an adequate
    rate of return for the owners. The combined rate neces-
    sary to cover the cost of debt and equity funds is
    referred to as the company's
    A. cost of capital   B. internal rate of return
    C. net present value   D. discount rate

18. Which of the following is NOT an advantage associated   18.___
    with short-term borrowing as opposed to other forms of
    financing?
    It
    A. helps establish a close relationship with banks
    B. has more flexibility
    C. typically involves no prepayment penalties
    D. can usually be used to take care of future needs

Questions 19-20.

DIRECTIONS: Questions 19 and 20 refer to the information below.

    Blake Industries' production process requires an average of
70 days to go from raw materials to finished products, and another
30 days before the finished goods are sold. Blake also extends
credit to customers and has an accounts receivable cycle of 58 days
based on its net sales. Materials for Blake are purchased on credit
from suppliers, and the accounts payable cycle averages 50 days
based on Blake's cost of goods sold.

19. What is Blake Industries' short-term operating cycle, in   19.___
    days?
    A. 100   B. 108   C. 158   D. 208

20. About how many times does Blake's short-term operating   20.___
    cycle turn over each year?
    A. 1.75   B. 2.31   C. 3.38   D. 3.65

21. Cost-push inflation typically occurs in response to   21.___
    A. lower wages accompanied by increased productivity
    B. higher production costs accompanied by increased
       productivity
    C. temporary resource shortages
    D. higher production costs without increased produc-
       tivity

22. What is the term for an initial sale of newly issued debt   22.___
    or equity securities?
    A. Flotation   B. Hedging
    C. Turnover   D. Intermediation

23. When the rate of return on borrowed funds is higher than   23.___
    their cost to a firm, _____ has occurred.
    A. negative financial leverage
    B. buying on margin
    C. positive financial leverage
    D. inflation

24. Which of the following is NOT a factor involved in deter-   24.___
    mining the expected return of a common stock?
    A. Growth   B. Present value
    C. Dividends   D. Stock price

25. Each of the following categories of risk is considered   25.___
    to affect the financing of business firms EXCEPT _____
    risk.
    A. transactions   B. macroeconomics business
    C. purchasing power   D. interest rate

——

KEY (CORRECT ANSWERS)

1. A		11. C	
2. B		12. D	
3. A		13. A	
4. B		14. C	
5. C		15. C	
6. A		16. B	
7. C		17. A	
8. A		18. D	
9. B		19. B	
10. A		20. C	

21. D
22. A
23. C
24. B
25. A

——

TEST 4

DIRECTIONS: Each question or incomplete statement is followed by several suggested answers or completions. Select the one that BEST answers the question or completes the statement. *PRINT THE LETTER OF THE CORRECT ANSWER IN THE SPACE AT THE RIGHT.*

1. In credit analysis, a borrower's financial ability to pay   1.____
   bills as they come due is described in terms of
      A. capital   B. collateral C. capacity D. character

2. Which of the following would NOT be considered a current   2.____
   liability for a business?
      A. Wages   B. Notes payable
      C. Mortgages   D. Interest

3. In general, stock prices change over time in response to   3.____
   changes in each of the following EXCEPT
      A. cash dividend levels
      B. weighted average cost of capital
      C. investor-expected returns
      D. growth rates

4. Which of the following typically constitutes the smallest   4.____
   proportion of a manufacturing firm's assets?
      A. Equipment and facilities
      B. Inventories
      C. Accounts receivable
      D. Cash and marketable securities

5. Which of the following typically accompanies a documentary   5.____
   draft in foreign exchange?
      A. Traveler's letter of credit
      B. Trust receipt
      C. Order bill of lading
      D. Manifest

6. A firm's inventory turnover is estimated by means of   6.____
      A. dividing inventories by accounts receivable
      B. dividing the cost of goods sold by inventories
      C. adding inventories and accounts receivable
      D. subtracting inventories from accounts receivable

7. A company is considering an investment project that is   7.____
   estimated to cost $8,000, and the incremental cost of
   capital is estimated at 12%. The investment cost will
   be incurred at the beginning of next year, and cash flows
   occur at the end of next year. The most likely cash flow
   for the coming year is estimated to be $10,000.
   If the term of the investment is a single year, what is
   the investment's net present value?
      A. -$857   B. $36   C. $929   D. $1,821

8. Which of the following business costs are primarily   8.__
   variable in nature?
   A. General and administrative expenses
   B. Cost of goods sold
   C. Interest expenses
   D. Depreciation expenses

9. For a corporation, the primary DISADVANTAGE associated   9.__
   with employing a liberal dividend policy is that it
   A. will lower the price of public issues of securities
   B. reduces internally generated funds available for
      investment
   C. increases the corporation's tax burden
   D. may appear unfavorable to stockholders

10. The most frequent justification given by lenders for   10.__
    requiring a compensating balance on unsecured loans is
    A. federal reserve requirements
    B. poor business credit
    C. inflation
    D. the inability to lend without deposits

11. What is the term for the promissory notes that can be   11.__
    issued or sold by large U.S. corporations of high credit
    quality?
    A. Acceptances   B. Lines of credit
    C. Commercial paper   D. Stock or bond power

12. According to the recommendations of the Bank Management   12.__
    Commission of the American Bankers Association, a loan
    based on the security of accounts receivable should
    generally be no more than ____% of the company's gross
    receivables.
    A. 60   B. 70   C. 80   D. 90

13. Which of the following is NOT an advantage associated   13.__
    with the use of bonds for financing, rather than stocks?
    A. *Cheaper-dollar* paybacks due to inflation
    B. Equity interests remain intact
    C. No sinking fund requirements
    D. Tax-deductible interest

14. The Joan Company sells on credit terms of net/60 days.   14.__
    Its net sales total $1.5 million, and its accounts
    receivable balance is $300,000.
    What is the average collection period for this company,
    in days?
    A. 50   B. 72   C. 138   D. 180

15. Foreign exchange markets are   15.__
    A. major financial centers linked by exceptional
       communications
    B. located at specific locations in major industrial
       cities

      C. facilities set up by central banks for foreign
         exchanges
      D. money markets located outside of the United States

16. When a long-term debt is due within _____ from the date   16.___
    of the current balance sheet, it is generally transferred
    to the current liabilities section.
    A. 90 days   B. 6 months   C. 1 year   D. 3 years

17. A bond issued by a company with significant financial   17.___
    problems should be considered by a financial manager
    as a _____ risk.
    A. purchasing power   B. default
    C. liquidity   D. market

18. In capital budgeting, the payback period method is used   18.___
    primarily to
    A. determine the present value interest factor for a
       particular investment
    B. compare two investments to determine which one
       recovers its initial outlay more quickly
    C. determine the maximum initial cash outlay for a
       particular investment
    D. determine whether a risk premium should be added to
       a company's cost of capital

19. When a parcel of real estate has more than one mortgage   19.___
    lien against it, the bonds outstanding against mortgages
    filed after the first mortgage are
    A. debenture bonds   B. second mortgage bonds
    C. junior liens   D. indentures

20. Which of the following is true of industries that   20.___
    experience only minor operating changes and reverses
    over the business cycle?
    A. They generally have less long-term debt than com-
       panies with dramatic cyclical swings.
    B. Their investments generally have a profitability
       index of greater than 2.
    C. They make greater use of factoring services than
       less stable firms.
    D. They generally make greater use of borrowed capital
       than firms with wide cyclical swings.

21. Which of the following should be used as a company's   21.___
    discount rate for making future capital budgeting
    decisions?
    The
    A. internal rate of return on its investment projects
    B. average yield to maturity of its investment projects
    C. weighted average cost of capital
    D. average face yield of its investment projects

22. The present value of an investment project is determined   22.__
by
A. dividing the initial outlay by the annual cash inflow of the investment
B. subtracting the initial outlay from the present value of all cash inflows for the life of the investment
C. dividing the initial outlay by the cash inflow annuity amount (annual receipt)
D. subtracting the initial outlay from the cash inflow annuity amount

Questions 23-25.

DIRECTIONS: Questions 23 through 25 refer to the information below.

The company Technosoft is considering the development, manufacture, and sale of product for $200 each. The variable costs (raw materials and direct labor) are estimated at $100 per copy, and the fixed costs allocated to this product would be $80,000.

23. If sales reach 1,000 units per year, what would be the   23.__
operating profits generated by this product
A. $10,000   B. $20,000   C. $35,000   D. $45,000

24. How many units of the product will need to be sold in   24.__
order for the company to break even?
A. 150   B. 200   C. 400   D. 800

25. Expressed in dollars, Technosoft's break-even point for   25.__
this product would be
A. $40,000   B. $80,000   C. $160,000   D. $180,000

KEY (CORRECT ANSWERS)

1. C		11. C	
2. C		12. C	
3. B		13. C	
4. D		14. B	
5. C		15. A	
6. B		16. C	
7. C		17. B	
8. B		18. B	
9. B		19. C	
10. D		20. D	

21. C
22. B
23. B
24. D
25. C

EXAMINATION SECTION
TEST 1

DIRECTIONS: Each question or incomplete statement is followed by several suggested answers or completions. Select the one that BEST answers the question or completes the statement. *PRINT THE LETTER OF THE CORRECT ANSWER IN THE SPACE AT THE RIGHT.*

1. The decision of whether to invest in a fixed asset begins with the
   A. determination of inventory turnover
   B. estimation of current assets
   C. determination of the maximum possible cost for investment
   D. development of a schedule of relevant cash flows

   1.___

2. The relation of net income to total assets reveals a(n) _____ ratio.
   A. profitability   B. asset utilization
   C. liquidity   D. financial leverage

   2.___

3. During the capital budgeting process, a risk-adjusted discount rate is most likely to be added to the company's cost of capital when estimating for
   A. the replacement of aging equipment used in production of existing products
   B. the best choice among equipment available from competing suppliers
   C. expansion projects involving new areas and product lines
   D. projects that are not in direct competition with one another

   3.___

4. Which of the following are disadvantages associated with the use of factoring services for short-term funding?
   I. Unknown costs of doing business through credit sales
   II. Higher overhead
   III. Relatively higher financing costs
   IV. The implication of financial weakness

   The CORRECT answer is:
   A. I, II   B. I, III   C. III, IV   D. I, II, IV

   4.___

5. *Convertible* preferred stock is so named because
   A. dividends can be transferred to invest in long-term debt funds at the stockholder's option
   B. it can be converted to common stock of the corporation at the stockholder's option
   C. it can be retired by the corporation at its option
   D. it carries a previously stated dividend

   5.___

6. The extent to which a company's assets are financed by   6.___
   liabilities is typically indicated by calculating the
   company's
   A. discount rate
   B. equity multiplier ratio
   C. negative financial leverage
   D. debt ratio

7. What is the term for credit extended to a business's   7.___
   customers for purchases of the company's products or
   services?
   A. Trade credit   B. Goodwill motive
   C. Purchase indemnity   D. Trade subsidy

8. A liquidity ratio that is calculated by dividing the   8.___
   residual of current assets minus inventories by the
   firm's current liabilities is referred to as a(n) _____
   ratio.
   A. cost-volume   B. acid-test
   C. asset turnover   D. equity

9. Each of the following is an advantage associated with   9.___
   the use of trade credit for short-term financing EXCEPT it
   A. is easy to obtain
   B. involves zero or minimal financing costs
   C. is easily convertible
   D. has no collateral requirements

10. When a loan is offered that is not a mortgage, what is   10.___
    typically used as security on real property?
    A. A deed of trust   B. All current assets
    C. A debenture bond   D. All fixed assets

11. The purpose of an income statement is to   11.___
    A. show the owners' equity accumulated as profits
       within the corporation
    B. show the assets and liabilities of a firm
    C. record cash received and disbursed
    D. itemize the net profit or loss of a firm during a
       specified time period

12. Which of the following types of drafts used in foreign   12.___
    exchanges requires immediate payment?
    _____ draft.
    A. Sight   B. Time
    C. Documentary   D. Clean

13. Generally, the purpose of financing some of a business's   13.___
    assets with long-term debt is to
    A. make use of current liabilities as well
    B. provide the owners with a rate of return on owners'
       equity that is higher than the rate of return on
       assets

C. provide the owners with a rate of return on owners' equity that is the same as the return to the owners

D. provide the owners with a rate of return on assets that is higher than the rate of return on owners' equity

14. The main limitation to the net present value method of capital budgeting is that it   14.___
    A. ignores all after-tax cash inflows
    B. does not consider the time value of money
    C. determines the annual receipt from the investment
    D. does not give the actual rates of return on the investment

15. Constant periodic annuity payments are most often deter-   15.___
    mined in association with
    A. irrevocable trusts   B. municipal bonds
    C. securities   D. amortized loans

16. Investors in a company expect to receive cash dividends   16.___
    next year of $4 per share. The common stock is currently
    selling for $60 a share. The stock value is expected to
    rise to $64 a share over the next year.
    What is the expected dividend yield?
    A. 3.3%   B. 6.7%   C. 11.1%   D. 15.0%

17. In determining the amount of new external funds needed   17.___
    to finance a company's asset additions, which of the
    following would be performed FIRST?
    A. Subtracting the expected amount of internally
       generated profits from the planned asset investments
    B. Subtracting the amount of spontaneous increases
       expected in accounts payable and accrued liabilities
       from the planned asset investments
    C. Forecasting the dollar amount of expected sales
       increase
    D. Determining the dollar amount of new asset invest-
       ments needed to support increased sales

18. If a corporation wants to obtain equity capital without   18.___
    diluting the control of current stockholders, it will
    typically
    A. reduce the work force   B. issue common stock
    C. finance with bonds   D. issue preferred stock

19. Which of the following is NOT in line with the principle   19.___
    of hedging?
    A. Fluctuating current assets associated with seasonal
       operations should be financed with short-term
       liabilities.
    B. Permanent current assets should be financed with
       short-term debt.
    C. Fixed assets should be financed with long-term debt
       and owners' equity funds.
    D. Assets should mature as liabilities mature.

20. The agency in most cities that is set up by consumer finance companies to provide information on loans is the credit

    A. union   B. league   C. exchange   D. bureau

21. Blake Industries' inventory turns over about 3.6 times a year, and its annual cost of goods sold is $450,000. Accounts receivable turns over on average 7 times a year. What would be the approximate average inventory on Blake's balance sheet?

    A. $64,285   B. $125,000   C. $231,430   D. $875,000

22. A company's balance sheet indicates the relationship of equality expressed as follows: Assets = Liabilities +

    A. Accounts payable   B. Owners' equity
    C. Net revenues   D. Working capital

23. Typically, a commercial finance company advances funds to businesses in each of the following ways EXCEPT

    A. discounting accounts receivable
    B. financing deferred-payment sales of commercial and industrial equipment
    C. discounting acceptances
    D. making loans secured by chattel mortgages on machinery or liens on inventory

24. Improving a company's asset turnover ratio involves _____ its percentage of _____.

    A. *decreasing*; sales to income
    B. *decreasing*; assets to sales
    C. *increasing*; sales to income
    D. *increasing*; assets to sales

25. Which of the following aspects of a business's internal and external financing is generally considered to be most important?

    A. The capital market
    B. The firm's dividend policy
    C. Par value of common stock
    D. Taxes

———

KEY (CORRECT ANSWERS)

1. D	6. D	11. D	16. B	21. B
2. A	7. A	12. A	17. C	22. B
3. C	8. B	13. B	18. D	23. C
4. C	9. C	14. D	19. B	24. B
5. B	10. A	15. D	20. C	25. B

———

TEST 2

DIRECTIONS: Each question or incomplete statement is followed by several suggested answers or completions. Select the one that BEST answers the question or completes the statement. *PRINT THE LETTER OF THE CORRECT ANSWER IN THE SPACE AT THE RIGHT.*

1. Accrued liabilities typically include the following EXCEPT
   A. interest on notes
   C. wages and salaries
   B. accounts payable
   D. taxes

   1.___

2. The contractual terms associated with a bond issue are spelled out in detail in a(n)
   A. trust indenture
   C. acceptance
   B. surety contract
   D. trust receipt

   2.___

Questions 3-5.

DIRECTIONS: Questions 3 through 5 refer to the information below.

A company's net sales for a single year total $1.4 million. Its variable costs, which the company keeps steady at 60% of net sales, totaled $840,000 and its fixed costs were $400,000.

3. What was the company's earnings before taxes?
   A. $160,000
   C. $560,000
   B. $440,000
   D. $1.4 million

   3.___

4. If the company's sales increase by 10% in the coming year, what would be the percent change in the company's operating income?
   A. -35%   B. 0%   C. +17.5%   D. +35%

   4.___

5. If the company's sales increase by 10%, what will be the company's degree of operating leverage?
   A. -3.5   B. 0   C. 1.75   D. 3.5

   5.___

6. A statement by a bank guaranteeing acceptance and payment of a draft up to a stated amount is called a(n)
   A. commercial letter of credit
   B. promissory note
   C. acceptance
   D. clean draft

   6.___

7. An annuity yields $1,000 a year for three years at a discount rate of 8%. The present value of the annuity is
   A. $2,382   B. $2,571   C. $2,577   D. $2,778

   7.___

8. Short-term promissory notes of commercial bank customers, which can be discounted with Federal Reserve banks, are known as
    A. commercial paper
    B. eligible paper
    C. clean drafts
    D. treasury notes

8.___

9. What type of financial ratio will be revealed by the turnover of accounts such as receivables and inventories?
    A. Asset utilization
    B. Liquidity
    C. Profitability
    D. Financial leverage

9.___

10. Which of the following offers the best explanation for why quotations of foreign exchange rates are identical (or nearly so) in cities worldwide?
    A. Price fixing
    B. Central bank control
    C. Arbitrage activities
    D. Travelers' letters of credit

10.___

11. A lender agrees to a $1,000 receipt -- ten years in the future -- for a loan offered at an 8% discount rate. What is the present value of the loan?
    A. $386
    B. $463
    C. $681
    D. $800

11.___

12. Which of the following is NOT a source of long-term financing?
    A. Equity securities
    B. Bonds
    C. Mortgages
    D. Commercial paper

12.___

13. A company's financial officer is using a profitability index to determine whether a project is a good candidate for investment. In order to be considered a good candidate, the project should have a profitability index of AT LEAST
    A. 0.25
    B. 0.5
    C. 1
    D. 2

13.___

Questions 14-15.

DIRECTIONS: Questions 14 and 15 refer to the information below.

A company plans to invest $100 each year for four years and will earn 10% per year.

14. If the first $100 is invested now, what will be the future value of the annuity?
    A. $146.40
    B. $464.10
    C. $510.50
    D. $610.50

14.___

15. If the company waits a year to make its first investment, what will be the future value of the annuity?
    A. $146.40
    B. $464.10
    C. $510.50
    D. $610.50

15.___

16. Which of the following are NOT direct equity claims?
    A. Options
    B. Warrants
    C. Preferred stocks
    D. Common stocks

16.___

17. A lender offers a $20,000, 10%, three-year loan that is   17.____
    to be fully amortized with three annual payments. The
    first payment will be due one year from the loan date.
    The present value interest factor (PVIFA) for 10% is 2.487.
    What is the approximate amount of each payment?
       A. $5,471.40 B. $7,333.33 C. $8,041.82 D. $8,846.00

18. Concentration risk refers to   18.____
       A. a lack of diversification in a company's investment
          portfolio
       B. factors such as financial condition and product
          demand that affect the value of an investment
       C. the variability in the value of an investment as
          interest rates, money market, or capital market
          conditions change
       D. the possibility that an investment may not be sold
          on short notice for its market value

19. Which of the following would be a typical use of a cash   19.____
    transaction statement?
       A. Measuring firm profitability as measured by the rate
          of return on assets
       B. Comparing the firm's ratios against industry ratios
       C. Showing the extent to which assets have been used
          to support revenue or sales
       D. Forecasting short-term borrowing needs

20. Which of the following stock market indicators relates   20.____
    the dispersion of general price fluctuation and is useful
    as an advance indicator of major price declines or
    advances?
       A. Relative strength analysis
       B. Trading volume
       C. Market breadth
       D. The *Barron's Confidence* index

21. A banker's acceptance   21.____
       A. depends entirely on the goodwill of the importer
       B. is always accompanied by a bank letter of credit
       C. is always less costly than a bill of exchange
       D. is not drawn on an importer

22. Which of the following U.S. Treasury obligations have   22.____
    the shortest maturities?
       A. Bills   B. Notes
       C. Certificates of deposit D. Bonds

Questions 23-25.

DIRECTIONS: Questions 23 through 25 refer to the information below.

    The James Manufacturing Company's financial statement results
for the previous year include the following: Net sales were $2
million with net income of $140,000. At year end, the total assets
of the company amounted to $1.6 million.

23. What is the company's profit margin?   23.__
    A. 6.75%   B. 7%   C. 8%   D. 8.75%

24. What is the company's asset turnover ratio?   24.__
    A. 0.33   B. 0.75   C. 1.25   D. 1.50

25. The company's return on its assets would be expressed   25.__
    as which of the following percentages?
    A. 7.5%   B. 8.75%   C. 10.5%   D. 18.0%

——

KEY (CORRECT ANSWERS)

1. B		11. B	
2. A		12. D	
3. A		13. C	
4. D		14. C	
5. D		15. B	
6. A		16. C	
7. C		17. C	
8. B		18. A	
9. A		19. D	
10. C		20. C	

21. D
22. A
23. B
24. C
25. B

——

TEST 3

Each question or incomplete statement is followed by several suggested answers or completions. Select the one that BEST answers the question or completes the statement. *PRINT THE LETTER OF THE CORRECT ANSWER IN THE SPACE AT THE RIGHT.*

1. The primary basis for a manufacturing firm's earning power or profitability is its
   A. working capital management
   B. liquidity ratio
   C. investment in current assets
   D. investment in fixed assets

   1.____

2. In terms of liquidity, quality, and marketability, which of the following tends to best serve businesses as a marketable security?
   A. Money market accounts
   B. U.S. Treasury bills
   C. Negotiable certificates of deposit (CDs)
   D. Commercial paper

   2.____

3. Which of the following is an organization that engages in accounts receivable financing by purchasing accounts and assuming all risks?
   A. Factor
   B. Commercial finance company
   C. Commercial bank
   D. Surety company

   3.____

Questions 4-5.

DIRECTIONS: Questions 4 and 5 refer to the information below.

The Laker Corporation's balance sheet reveals that the company's assets total $1 million. Its liabilities total $450,000. The owners' equity totals $550,000.

4. What is the Laker Corporation's debt ratio?
   A. 0.33   B. 0.45   C. 0.55   D. 0.82

   4.____

5. What is the Laker Corporation's equity multiplier ratio?
   A. 0.45   B. 0.82   C. 1.82   D. 2.22

   5.____

6. Most often, the largest single current liability of a business is
   A. the tax accrual   B. wages and salaries
   C. accounts payable   D. notes payable

   6.____

7. Investors in a company expect a 12.5% rate of return on their common stock. The expected growth rate is 7.5% annually, and the stock is expected to pay $4 in cash dividends next year. What is the present value of the stock?
   A. $20   B. $40   C. $60   D. $80   7.__

8. Bonds which are dependent upon the general credit and strength of the corporation for their security are referred to as _____ bonds.   8.__
   A. tied   B. creditor
   C. debenture   D. property-dependent

Questions 9-10.

DIRECTIONS: Questions 9 and 10 refer to the information below.

   Spacely, Inc. has total current assets of $500,000 and total current liabilities of $250,000. Its inventories also total $250,000.

9. What is Spacely's current ratio?   9.__
   A. 1:3   B. 1:2   C. 1:1   D. 2:1

10. What is Spacely's acid-test ratio?   10.__
   A. 1:3   B. 1:2   C. 1:1   D. 2:1

11. Under current tax law, businesses are allowed to depreciate _____% of their fixed assets in the seven-year property class during the first year.   11.__
   A. 4   B. 9   C. 14   D. 25

12. What is the purpose of calculating a company's degree of operating leverage?   12.__
   A. Determining the decrease or increase in sales
   B. Determining fixed costs as a percentage of sales
   C. Quantifying the responsiveness of operating expenses to the level of output
   D. Quantifying the responsiveness of operating income to the level of output

13. A firm's ability to generate earnings adequate to pay cash dividends and allow for some earnings retention is influenced to a large extent by the firm's   13.__
   A. net revenue   B. inventories
   C. profit margin   D. asset turnover

14. An asset in the form of money due to a firm by a certain date is known as a(n)   14.__
   A. note receivable   B. fixed asset
   C. account receivable   D. intangible asset

15. In general, the activity considered to be of greatest importance to most financial officers is   15.__
   A. receivables management
   B. planning and budgeting
   C. debt valuation
   D. working capital management

16. What is the term for a type of receivable instrument that   16.___
    arises out of the sale of merchandise to a business
    customer and which may be sold to a bank?
       A. Acceptance   B. Outlay
       C. Market order   D. Commercial paper

17. When a financial analyst looks at the direction and magni- 17.___
    tude of the market in terms of what to buy or sell, a(n)
    _____ analysis is being conducted.
       A. technical   B. time series
       C. off-budget   D. trend

18. Internally generated funds for financing new asset   18.___
    investments come generally from
       A. long-term debt   B. short-term debt
       C. equity funds   D. profits

Questions 19-20.

DIRECTIONS: Questions 19 and 20 refer to the information below.

    The Kingsley Group is considering the purchase of a hammermill
for a total cost of $40,000 that will have a five-year life before
it is discarded. Cash revenues from the sale of inventories are
expected to be $24,000 a year, and cash operating expenses associated
with the use of the hammermill are estimated at $11,200 per year.
The company, which is in the 25% tax bracket, is entitled to
depreciate the hammermill for income tax purposes -- assume that the
company takes advantage of this deduction.

19. What will be the Kingsley Group's annual after-tax cash   19.___
    earnings if the hammermill is purchased?
       A. $2,800   B. $3,600   C. $4,800   D. $8,000

20. What would be the company's annual cash inflow after   20.___
    taxes?
       A. $5,600   B. $8,000   C. $11,600   D. $12,200

21. In order to determine an investment's present value, it   21.___
    is sometimes necessary to translate future cash benefits
    to the present. This process is known as
       A. remission   B. discounting
       C. rebating   D. hedging

22. Which stage in the capital budgeting process typically   22.___
    involves the estimation of relevant cash inflows and
    outflows?
       A. Development   B. Implementation
       C. Identification   D. Selection

23. In a financial leverage ratio, total liabilities are   23.___
    often expressed as a percentage of
       I. stockholders' equity
      II. total assets
     III. Net income

The CORRECT answer is:
A. I *only*   B. I, II   C. II *only*   D. II, III

24. What is the term for an instrument through which a bank   24.___
    retains title to goods until they are paid for?
    A. Time draft   B. Arbitrage
    C. Trust receipt   D. Documentary draft

25. It is generally true that as price levels increase, the   25.___
    increased costs for a business will be offset to the
    extent that
    A. current assets are financed by current or long-term
       borrowing
    B. the rate of asset turnover is increased
    C. its products remain competitive
    D. accounts receivable hold stable

———

KEY (CORRECT ANSWERS)

1. D		11. C	
2. B		12. D	
3. A		13. C	
4. B		14. A	
5. C		15. B	
6. A		16. A	
7. D		17. A	
8. C		18. D	
9. D		19. B	
10. C		20. C	

21. B
22. A
23. B
24. C
25. A

———

TEST 4

DIRECTIONS: Each question or incomplete statement is followed by several suggested answers or completions. Select the one that BEST answers the question or completes the statement. *PRINT THE LETTER OF THE CORRECT ANSWER IN THE SPACE AT THE RIGHT.*

1. Practically all modern preferred stock is   1.___
   A. callable   B. noncumulative
   C. convertible   D. cumulative

2. In general, the profitability of a firm is affected to   2.___
   the greatest extent by the success of its financial
   manager in
   A. making current asset investment decisions
   B. creating a capital budget
   C. making fixed-asset investment decisions
   D. avoiding long-term liabilities

3. Which of the following is/are ways in which the Small   3.___
   Business Administration assists in the financing of small
   businesses?
     I. Guaranteeing bank loans to businesses
    II. Participating jointly with banks in extending loans
        to businesses
   III. Making direct loans to businesses

   The CORRECT answer is:
   A. I *only*   B. I, II   C. II, III   D. I, II, III

4. Over time, a company's level of investment in fixed assets   4.___
   will be consistent with
   A. working capital   B. mortgage debt
   C. inventories   D. sales

5. Macroeconomic business risk is reflected in   5.___
   A. the importance of key employees
   B. short-term financing policies
   C. the degree of variability in a firm's sales and profits
   D. interest rates

6. The main DISADVANTAGE of using debt capital over equity   6.___
   capital is
   A. fewer special provisions such as conversion rights
   B. lower priority in the case of liquidation
   C. little or no control over firm activities
   D. generally lower yields

7. The process of using debt funds in an effort to increase   7.___
   the rate of return to owners or stockholders is
      A. trading on equity
      B. determining the weighted cost of capital
      C. buying on margin
      D. determining optimal capital structure

8. A company's marketable securities are held primarily to   8.___
   meet _____ motives.
      A. capacity   B. speculative
      C. precautionary   D. transactions

9. When the cash flow stream of an investment is constant or   9.___
   level in each time period, the investment is called a(n)
      A. annuity   B. real asset
      C. floater   D. trust

10. Which of the following is NOT a disadvantage associated   10.___
    with short-term borrowing as opposed to other forms of
    financing?
      A. Added element of financial risk
      B. Possibility of rising borrowing costs
      C. It tends to create inflexible operations
      D. Frequent renewals

11. The comparison of a firm's financial ratios over several   11.___
    years is known as a(n)
      A. statement of cash flows
      B. industry comparative analysis
      C. asset turnover statement
      D. trend analysis

12. In terms of a company's investment portfolio, changes in   12.___
    stock prices would be discussed as _____ risk.
      A. market   B. liquidity C. business   D. default

13. When determining whether or not to extend credit to a   13.___
    business, creditors generally place the greatest emphasis
    on
      A. total fixed assets   B. net working capital
      C. retained earnings   D. the prime rate

14. Secured long-term debt obligations are generally referred 14.___
    to as
      A. debenture bonds   B. mortgage bonds
      C. callable bonds   D. tied loans

15. Which of the following capital budgeting techniques does   15.___
    not explicitly consider the time value of money?
      A. Internal rate of return B. Net present value
      C. Payback period   D. Profitability index

16. When an investment earns interest that is reinvented   16.___
    along with the principal, _____ occurs.
       A. discounting   B. splitting
       C. compounding   D. special assessment

17. In risk-return analysis, standard deviation is used to   17.___
    measure the
       A. average dispersion of individual cash flows
       B. net present value of an investment
       C. expected value of the cash flows
       D. weighted cost of the investment

18. Which of the following type of business is characterized 18.___
    by relatively high current asset to fixed asset mixes?
       A. Retail store   B. Electric power
       C. Manufacturing   D. Railroad

19. A borrower offers to pay a lender $1,000 at the end of one 19.___
    year in return for a loan of $1,000 now. The lender
    agrees to receive exactly $1,000 a year from now, but
    insists on an 8% return on the loan.
    What amount would be lended?
       A. $800   B. $909   C. $926   D. $1,000

20. Which of the following types of corporations tend to rely 20.___
    almost exclusively on internally generated funds for
    financing?
       A. Corporations that invest heavily in fixed assets
       B. Rapidly growing firms such as high-technology firms
       C. Companies with high capital needs
       D. Corporations that require little investment in fixed
          assets

21. In the case of corporations, the owners' equity is   21.___
    usually broken down into several accounts. Which of the
    following is NOT one of these accounts?
       A. Capital earnings   B. Retained earnings
       C. Transfer payments   D. Common stock account

22. What type of long-term debt instrument allows for con-   22.___
    tinuing sale of bonds secured by the same mortgage?
       A. Closed-end mortgage bond
       B. Debenture bond
       C. Open-end mortgage bond
       D. Trust indenture

23. Each of the following are thrift institutions EXCEPT   23.___
       A. mutual savings banks
       B. commercial finance companies
       C. savings and loan associations
       D. credit unions

24. Whenever a company cannot or will not undertake all investment projects with a net present value greater than or equal to zero, _____ occurs.
    A. capital rationing
    C. hedging
    B. discounting
    D. sensitivity analysis

24.___

25. If a business relied entirely on short-term financing for its current asset requirements, the total current assets of the firm would
    A. be equal to the total current liabilities
    B. be less than the total current liabilities
    C. remain unchanged
    D. fluctuate depending on inventories

25.___

———

KEY (CORRECT ANSWERS)

1. B	11. D
2. C	12. A
3. D	13. B
4. D	14. B
5. C	15. C
6. D	16. C
7. A	17. A
8. C	18. A
9. A	19. C
10. C	20. D

21. C
22. C
23. B
24. A
25. A

———

EXAMINATION SECTION

DIRECTIONS: Each question or incomplete statement is followed by several suggested answers or completions. Select the one that BEST answers the question or completes the statement. *PRINT THE LETTER OF THE CORRECT ANSWER IN THE SPACE AT THE RIGHT.*

Questions 1-4.

DIRECTIONS: In answering Questions 1 through 4, select from the following five definitions the MOST appropriate answer to match each of the terms that follow.

    A. One who holds cash and securities for an investment company
    B. One who is engaged in the business of buying and selling securities for his own account and risk
    C. One who contracts with a prospective securities issuer to buy the issue at a specified price (firm commitment), or sell it on behalf of the issuer (best efforts)
    D. One who joins in a distribution of a securities issue and is committed financially only for those securities for which he elects to subscribe
    E. One who buys and sells securities for the account and risk of others and may charge a commission for his services

1. Underwriter   1.___

2. Selling group member   2.___

3. Dealer   3.___

4. Broker   4.___

5. A *subject market* is a   5.___
    A. quotation in which the prices are subject to confirmation
    B. quotation subject to change only on advance notice
    C. general term covering the subjects under discussion
    D. market in which subject securities are bought and sold
    E. market in which all transactions are subject to cancellation

6. The phrase *to make a market* means a(n)   6.___
    A. dealer creates and maintains a market in a security
    B. underwriter has made a new issue of securities available to the securities market
    C. group of local brokers and dealers have formed a new market or exchange in a city

D. firm has opened a new office in an area which formerly had no investment services available to it
E. none of the above

7. As used in over-the-counter quotations, the *spread* is   7.___
   A. the ratio between funds dealers invest in their business and amounts of borrowed capital
   B. the number of different securities issues traded
   C. the difference between bid and asked prices
   D. an arbitrage
   E. a term relating to a dealer's branch offices

8. The difference between the bid price and the asked price   8.___
in any quotation is called the
   A. remainder   B. profit   C. loss
   D. spread   E. commission

9. Such expressions as *and accrued interest*, *plus accrued*,   9.___
with accrued, *with interest*, etc., when applied to prices
given on interest-bearing securities, signify that
   A. the buyer will get some extra cash on delivery
   B. the dealer has his customers' interest in mind
   C. the dealer is particularly interested in the security
   D. accrued interest from the last payment date must be added to the dollar price of the securities
   E. none of the above

Questions 10-13.

DIRECTIONS: In answering Questions 10 through 13, select from the following five definitions the MOST appropriate answer to match each of the terms that follow.

   A. Day on which transaction is made between two parties
   B. Day on which securities must be delivered and paid for
   C. Day on and after which the buyer of a common stock is not entitled to a previously declared dividend
   D. Day on which is compiled a list of stockholders who will receive dividends from a corporation
   E. Day on which a dividend is paid by a corporation

10. Record date   10.__

11. Ex-dividend date   11.__

12. Trade date   12.__

13. Payable date   13.__

14. The term *good delivery*, when used in connection with a   14.__
security, means
   A. the delivery was accomplished and a signed receipt was obtained
   B. a security in such form that record ownership may readily be transferred

C. the ownership of the security has been transferred
D. the security has been received by the purchaser
E. none of the above

15. Which one of the following items is NOT to be found in or determined from the balance sheet of a corporation?
   A. Assets   B. Liabilities
   C. Net worth   D. Net income
   E. Working capital

15.___

16. The assets of a business are the
   A. amounts the business owes others
   B. items of value owned by the business
   C. profits not distributed to owners
   D. equity of the owners of the business
   E. none of the above

16.___

17. Which of the following is NOT an asset?
   A. Cash on hand
   B. Inventory
   C. Common stock issued and outstanding
   D. Marketable securities
   E. Accounts receivable

17.___

18. A corporation's intangible assets would include
   A. brand names   B. goodwill
   C. trademarks   D. patents owned
   E. all of the above

18.___

19. Liabilities are amounts owed by a business.
   Which of the following would NOT properly be considered a liability?
   A. Accrued wages
   B. Accounts payable
   C. Funded debt
   D. Reserve for accrued taxes
   E. Reserve for depreciation

19.___

20. Which of the following could NOT be included when referring to funded debt?
   A. $6\frac{1}{2}\%$ refunding bonds due 1994
   B. Mortgage on plant and equipment
   C. Serial bank notes due 1986 to 1998
   D. Class *A* preferred stock
   E. Equipment trust certificates

20.___

21. Capital or paid-in surplus includes
   A. excess funds held for a contingency
   B. earnings retained in the corporation
   C. amount paid into corporation by investors at time of issuance of capital stock in excess of par or stated value of shares issued
   D. excess of revenue earned over expenses incurred
   E. capital gains achieved in a corporation's investment account

21.___

22. The ABC Corporation has common and preferred stock out-
standing, funded debt and earned and capital surplus.
The sum of which of these would be referred to as the
capital structure of this corporation?
Common
   A. stock outstanding
   B. and preferred stock outstanding
   C. and preferred stock outstanding and funded debt
   D. and preferred stock outstanding, funded debt, and
      earned surplus
   E. and preferred stock outstanding, funded debt, and
      earned and capital surplus

22.___

23. Which of the following is NOT a part of a corporation's
capital structure?
   A. Common stock outstanding
   B. Preferred stock outstanding
   C. Bonds outstanding
   D. Capital or earned surplus
   E. Authorized, but unissued, stock

23.___

24. Current ratio is the ratio of
   A. liabilities to assets
   B. assets to liabilities
   C. cash on hand to net worth
   D. current assets to current liabilities
   E. difference between current assets and current
      liabilities

24.___

25. Net working capital is defined as
   A. the amount invested in securities
   B. excess of assets over liabilities
   C. a ratio of funds invested in business
   D. excess of current assets over current liabilities
   E. total amount of funds *at work* in the business

25.___

26. In the securities business, the term *leverage* means
   A. a means of obtaining faster price action
   B. the employment of borrowed money or senior capital
      under circumstances that provide for the common
      stock of a company opportunity for greater earnings
      and/or appreciation, accompanied by a correspondingly
      greater degree of risk
   C. a measure of the market demand necessary to move the
      price of a stock 1 point
   D. the action taken by floor specialists to prevent
      securities prices from declining unduly
   E. a procedure which enables one to corner the market
      in a security

26.___

27. Someone about to make an investment in common stocks
should always consider his alternatives in relation to
several factors.
Which of the following need NOT be a factor to be considered by the investor?

27.___

A. Safety
C. Income
E. Par or stated value
B. Marketability or liquidity
D. Appreciation

Questions 28-31.

DIRECTIONS: In answering Questions 28 through 31, select from the following five definitions the MOST appropriate answer to match each of the terms that follow.

A. Relative ability to convert investment to cash or a cash equivalent
B. Increase in market price of investment
C. Return on investment
D. Hazard of loss of all or part of investment
E. Process of selecting an investment

28. Risk   28.____

29. Liquidity   29.____

30. Appreciation   30.____

31. Income or yield   31.____

Questions 32-35.

DIRECTIONS: In answering Questions 32 through 35, select from the following five definitions the MOST appropriate answer to match each of the terms that follow.

A. An investment company whose stated policy is at all times to have some portion of its invested assets in bonds and preferred stocks, as well as in common stocks
B. An investment company whose stated objective is to seek long-term growth of capital by investing in the securities of companies which plow back a substantial part of earnings for expansion, research or development purposes
C. An investment company with a fixed number of shares of stock outstanding, which are traded as ordinary corporate securities
D. An investment company whose stated management objective is maximum current income
E. An investment company which invests in the securities of companies in a single industry or in allied industries

32. Income fund   32.____

33. Specialty fund   33.____

34. Balanced fund   34.____

35. Growth fund   35.____

36. Institutions interested in large blocks of securities do   36.___
a substantial portion of their business in the over-the-
counter market because
    A. government and municipal bonds trade principally in
       the over-the-counter market
    B. new issues are first available in volume in the over-
       the-counter market
    C. they can buy and sell in the over-the-counter market
       without unduly affecting the price
    D. if redistribution of a very large block is necessary,
       it can usually be accomplished more effectively in
       the over-the-counter market
    E. all of the above

37. In general, a short sale refers to the sale of   37.___
    A. fewer shares than usually considered the trading
       unit of any given security
    B. securities by two principals without the help of an
       intervening broker
    C. securities held less than 6 months
    D. securities which are not owned by the seller
    E. securities for less than $1.00 per share

38. The document that MUST be delivered to buyers of   38.___
registered securities under the Securities Act of 1933 is
the
    A. annual report   B. commission schedule
    C. prospectus   D. certificate of membership
    E. financial statement

39. The Securities Exchange Act of 1934, as amended, provides,   39.___
among other things, for
    A. regulation and registration of securities exchanges
    B. regulation of the over-the-counter market
    C. regulation of brokers and dealers
    D. registration of national securities associations
    E. all of the above

40. Under a rule of the SEC (240.17a-5), registered broker/   40.___
dealers are required to file financial statements with
the Commission
    A. when most convenient to their way of doing business
    B. quarterly
    C. semi-annually
    D. once each calendar year
    E. only while solvent

41. Under Rule 144 of the Securities Act of 1933, as amended,   41.___
which of the following is(are) TRUE?
    I. Rule concerns the purchaser of restricted or letter
      stock
   II. There is a two-year holding period
  III. Rule concerns the issuer of letter or restricted stock
   IV. Only a limited amount of securities may be sold once
     every 3 months

The CORRECT answer is:
A. I *only*   B. III, IV   C. I, IV
D. I, II, IV   E. III *only*

42. The common name applied to legislation that regulates the   42.___
sale of securities in certain states is
A. Gresham's Law   B. Blue Laws
C. Blue Sky Laws   D. Law of Supply and Demand
E. Internal Revenue Code

43. What agency prescribes regulations with respect to the   43.___
extension of credit by brokers and dealers?
A. Federal Trade Commission
B. National Association of Securities Dealers, Inc.
C. Treasury Department
D. Federal Reserve Board
E. Farm Credit Administration

44. An explanation of the risk of market fluctuation that is   44.___
involved in investment company shares is required when
which of the following is discussed?
A. Appreciation and profit possibilities
B. Preservation of capital
C. Protection against loss of purchasing power or
   accumulation of an estate
D. Diversification of investment
E. Any of the above

45. What is the National Association of Securities Dealers,   45.___
Inc.?
A
A. trade association to stimulate investing by the public
B. service club for brokers and dealers
C. registered national securities association empowered
   by Federal law to require its members to maintain
   high standards of commercial honor and just and
   equitable principles of trade
D. branch of the SEC that checks up on the securities
   business
E. none of the above

46. Which of the following is NOT one of the Association's   46.___
functions?
To
A. promote the investment banking and securities business,
   standardize its principles and practices, promote high
   standards of commercial honor and observance of
   Federal and state securities laws
B. provide a medium through which its membership can be
   enabled to confer, consult, and cooperate with governmental and other agencies in the solution of problems
   affecting investors, the public, and the investment
   banking and securities business
C. promote better profits and commissions for over-the-
   counter dealers and Registered Representatives

D. adopt, administer, and enforce rules of fair practice and rules to prevent fraudulent and manipulative acts and practices and, in general, to promote just and equitable principles of trade for the protection of investors

E. promote self-discipline among members, and to investigate and adjust grievances between the public and members and between members

47. Which of these is NOT eligible for Association membership, except by order of the Securities and Exchange Commission? A broker/dealer   47.___

A. who has been expelled from the Association or from a registered national securities exchange

B. whose registration with the Securities and Exchange Commission has been revoked

C. who has been named a *cause* of an expulsion or revocation, or one whose registration as a Registered Representative has been revoked by the Association or by a registered national securities exchange

D. who has been convicted within the preceding ten years of any crime arising out of the securities business or involving embezzlement, fraudulent conversion, misappropriation of funds, or the abuse or misuse of a fiduciary relationship

E. all of the above

48. The Board of Governors may prescribe penalties applicable to members and/or Registered Representatives, for violation of the Association rules, including   48.___

A. censure
B. fines and costs of proceedings
C. suspension
D. expulsion
E. all of the above

49. A member participating in an initial offering of a security who fails to make a bona fide public offering of the security and instead retains his allotment for himself or his family or his employees or employee profit sharing plan is said to be   49.___

A. straddling
C. free riding
E. arbitraging
B. beating the bid
D. churning

50. The controlling factor when offering securities to an investor should be the interest   50.___

A. on the investment
C. of the firm
E. none of the above
B. of the salesman
D. of the investor

KEY (CORRECT ANSWERS)

1. C	11. C	21. C	31. C	41. D
2. D	12. A	22. E	32. D	42. C
3. B	13. E	23. E	33. E	43. D
4. E	14. B	24. D	34. A	44. E
5. A	15. D	25. D	35. D	45. C
6. A	16. B	26. B	36. E	46. C
7. C	17. C	27. E	37. D	47. E
8. D	18. E	28. D	38. C	48. E
9. D	19. E	29. A	39. E	49. C
10. D	20. D	30. B	40. D	50. D

EXAMINATION SECTION

DIRECTIONS: Each question or incomplete statement is followed by several suggested answers or completions. Select the one that BEST answers the question or completes the statement. *PRINT THE LETTER OF THE CORRECT ANSWER IN THE SPACE AT THE RIGHT.*

1. Common and/or preferred stock is(are) issued by which of   1.___
   the following?
   A
     A. business   B. partnership   C. proprietorship
     D. corporation   E. all of the above

2. Common stock represents _____ a corporation.   2.___
     A. a debt of   B. an asset of
     C. an ownership in   D. the net worth of
     E. a dividend from

3. Treasury stock is   3.___
     A. unissued stock
     B. authorized stock
     C. stock of a subsidiary, held by the treasurer
     D. stock which has been issued and reacquired by the
        issuer
     E. cancelled stock

4. Dividends are   4.___
     A. a distribution of debts
     B. contractual payments required of all corporations
     C. pro rata distributions among outstanding shares,
        usually paid in cash
     D. adjustments necessary to change the par value of
        common or preferred stock
     E. interest paid to common stockholders on the basis
        of shares owned

5. Sometimes a corporation pays a dividend in shares of its   5.___
   stock rather than in cash because
     A. the dividend is not taxable to the shareholders
     B. such dividends may be used to capitalize surplus
     C. the corporation wishes to conserve cash for its
        operations
     D. one of the corporation's objectives is to achieve
        broader distribution of its shares
     E. any of the above

6. _____ stock has first claim on any earnings available for   6.___
   dividends.
     A. Treasury   B. Common   C. Preferred
     D. Unissued   E. Exchange

7. A type of preferred stock on which dividends may exceed   7.__
   the specified rate is a
   A. discount preferred stock
   B. cumulative preferred stock
   C. preferred stock with rights attached
   D. convertible preferred stock
   E. participating preferred stock

8. Usually, back dividends on _____ stock must be declared   8.__
   before common stockholders may expect to receive cash
   dividends.
   A. preferred   B. participating preferred
   C. cumulative preferred   D. treasury
   E. convertible

9. The participating clause of a preferred stock provides   9.__
   that the holder has the
   A. right to convert the preferred stock into some other
      security issued by the corporation
   B. right to receive a stipulated dividend and then share
      in the earnings or dividends at a specified rate
      along with the common stockholders
   C. same voting rights available to the common stock-
      holders
   D. right to participate in management of the corporation
   E. right to participate in annual meetings

10. The redemption clause of a preferred stock provides that   10.__
    the
    A. holder receives a stipulated dividend and then shares
       in the earnings available for the common stockholders
    B. holder has preference as to assets over the common
       stockholders in the event of liquidation
    C. company may call in the stock and redeem it at a
       specified price
    D. holder has the right to convert the preferred stock
       into some other security issued by the corporation
    E. stock may be redeemed by the holder at his original
       cost at any time

Questions 11-14.

DIRECTIONS: In answering Questions 11 through 14, select from the
              following five definitions lettered A, B, C, D, and E
              the MOST appropriate answer to match each of the terms
              that follow.

          A. May be redeemed by the holder at original cost at
             any time
          B. Stock which has been issued and re-acquired by the
             issuer
          C. Represents ownership in a corporation
          D. Has prior claim over common stock in a distribution
             of the earnings of a corporation
          E. Physical evidence of ownership in a corporation

11. Treasury stock   11.___

12. Capital stock   12.___

13. Stock certificate   13.___

14. Preferred stock   14.___

Questions 15-18.

DIRECTIONS: In answering Questions 15 through 18, select from the
             following five definitions lettered A, B, C, D, and E
             the MOST appropriate answer to match each of the terms
             that follow.

15. Participating preferred stock   15.___

16. Convertible preferred stock   16.___

17. Callable preferred stock   17.___

18. Cumulative preferred stock   18.___

19. Bonds which are issued upon the general credit of the   19.___
    issuer and are NOT secured are termed _____ bonds.
       A. participating   B. consolidated mortgage
       C. adjustment   D. debenture
       E. convertible

20. A guaranteed corporate bond is one that is guaranteed as 20.___
    to principal and/or interest by
       A. the Securities and Exchange Commission
       B. the National Association of Securities Dealers, Inc.
       C. the New York Stock Exchange
       D. some one other than the issuer
       E. the United States Treasury

21. Bonds which are secured by other securities placed with 21.___
    a trustee are termed _____ bonds.
       A. mortgage   B. collateral trust
       C. debenture   D. guaranteed
       E. exempt

22. Bonds which contain a definite promise to pay the prin- 22.___
    cipal amount, with interest to be paid only when and if
    earned, are GENERALLY termed _____ bonds.
       A. income or adjustment   B. participating
       C. serial   D. debenture
       E. exempt

23. An income bond is one that   23.___
       A. has no claim on income of the issuing corporation
       B. guarantees a specific amount of income annually

C. provides a fixed rate of income return
D. is rated as Triple-A
E. may be secured as to principal, but has claim for interest only in the event of available income

Questions 24-27.

DIRECTIONS: In answering Questions 24 through 27, select from the following five terms the MOST appropriate answer to match each of the definitions that follow.

    A. Mortgage bond
    B. Debenture
    C. Revenue bond
    D. Income bond
    E. Collateral trust bond

24. An evidence of indebtedness which is secured by a lien on some underlying real property of a corporation.   24.__

25. An evidence of indebtedness which is secured by other securities placed with a trustee.   25.__

26. An evidence of indebtedness which is NOT secured by physical property but is issued upon the general credit of the issuer.   26.__

27. An evidence of indebtedness, the interest on which is normally paid only out of current earnings of the issuer.   27.__

Questions 28-31.

DIRECTIONS: In answering Questions 28 through 31, select from the following five terms the MOST appropriate answer to match each of the definitions that follow.

28. A bond with coupons attached which may be presented for payment of interest.   28.__

29. A bond of an issue which matures in part at stated intervals.   29.__

30. A bond which has the name of the owner recorded on the books of the issuer or its agent.   30.__

31. A bond which is retired by call or open market purchase from funds set aside in accordance with terms of an indenture.   31.__

32. General obligations of states and municipalities generally   32.___
carry a lower interest rate than corporate bonds for many
reasons. One reason is the theoretical safety of princi-
pal due to the issuers' power to tax.
Another reason is that
   A. such bonds have never defaulted
   B. investors feel they are doing a public service in
     buying them
   C. interest earned by the holder of such bonds is not
     presently subject to Federal income taxes and to
     state and local income taxes if holder resides in
     the state
   D. profits gained in the sale of such bonds are not
     subject to Federal income taxes
   E. municipalities cannot afford higher interest rates

33. What is the difference between United States Treasury   33.___
bonds and United States Treasury notes?
   A. None
   B. Bonds are issued as longer-term obligations - more
     than 5 years
   C. Notes are more volatile
   D. Both B and C are correct
   E. Bonds are guaranteed by the Treasury of the United
     States

34. ABC Corporation $100 par common stock is currently selling   34.___
for $75. The corporation has earned $5 per share in the
past year and has paid quarterly dividends as follows:
    March $.50, June $.17, Sept. $.75, Dec. $1.00
Based on the last four dividends, the current return for
the period is
   A. 5%   B. 5 1/3%   C. 6 2/3%   D. 4%   E. 3%

35. CDE Corporation $50 par common stock is currently selling   35.___
for $80. The corporation has earned $5 per share in the
past year and has paid quarterly dividends as follows:
    March $.75, June $.75, Sept. $1.00, Dec. $1.50
To find the current annual return, divide
   A. $4 by $80   B. $5 by $80   C. $6 by $80
   D. $4 by $50   E. $5 by $50

36. What is the current return (or yield) on a $100 par, $5   36.___
preferred stock selling at $125?
   A. 6.25%   B. 5.00%
   C. 4.00%   D. 2.50%
   E. None of the above

37. Five years ago, John Jones purchased 100 shares of AB Co.   37.___
common ($50 par) for $20 per share. In the year just past,
AB Co. common paid dividends of $2.00 per share and is
now selling for $100 per share.
The current return at the present market price is
   A. 2%   B. 4%
   C. 10%   D. 500%
   E. None of the above

38. KLM Bonds which have a 9.5% coupon rate and mature in   38.__
    5 years at par (100) are now selling at 90.
    The yield to maturity is found by dividing
        A. $9.50 by 100   B. $10.00 by 5
        C. $10.00 by 100   D. $9.50 by 90
        E. None of the above

39. A written authorization allowing another person to vote   39.__
    in the place of a stockholder is a
        A. proxy   B. right
        C. warrant   D. indenture
        E. protective covenant

Questions 40-43.

DIRECTIONS: In answering Questions 40 through 43, select from the
             following five definitions the MOST appropriate answer
             to match each of the terms that follow.

        A. A document representing the authorization to vote
           stock
        B. A document, sometimes attached to a security,
           representing a privilege to buy securities at a
           specified price
        C. A privilege granted to stockholders to subscribe at
           a specified price to additional securities in a
           forthcoming offering
        D. A document representing stock deposited under a
           voting trust
        E. A document representing an individual's promise to
           purchase common stock at the time a corporation is
           organized

40. Right   40.__

41. Proxy   41.__

42. Voting trust certificate   42.__

43. Warrant   43.__

44. Which of these securities are USUALLY traded over-the-   44.__
    counter?
        A. Bank and insurance company stocks
        B. Government and municipal bonds
        C. Investment company shares
        D. Guaranteed railroad securities
        E. All of the above

45. A(n) _____ buys and sells only for the account and risk   45.__
    of others.
        A. underwriter   B. dealer
        C. selling group member   D. broker
        E. trader

46. An issuer is a
    A. company which raises capital by issuing securities
    B. company which buys from the underwriter
    C. managing underwriter
    D. promoter-sponsor
    E. none of the above

    46.___

47. The function of the _____ is to negotiate with a prospective securities issuer and, after the terms of the offering have been agreed upon, to buy the issue at a specified price (firm commitment), or sell it on behalf of the issuer (best efforts).
    A. trader   B. dealer
    C. selling group member   D. underwriter
    E. broker

    47.___

48. Among the PRINCIPAL functions of the investment banker are to
    A. buy securities from an issuer and sell them to the public
    B. distribute large blocks of securities held by a few persons or a single large owner
    C. provide the means for raising new capital for industry
    D. buy and distribute securities of Federal and state governments and of municipalities
    E. all of the above

    48.___

49. A _____ joins in a distribution of a securities issue and is committed to purchase only the securities that are allotted to him at the time of the offering.
    A. specialist   B. dealer
    C. selling group member   D. broker
    E. trader

    49.___

50. As the term is applied to a quotation for a stock or a bond, a *firm* market is
    A. the market maintained by a firm in a particular security
    B. a market which is steady and not fluctuating rapidly
    C. the actual prices at which a security may be purchased or sold
    D. the trading room or market place of a particular firm
    E. none of the above

    50.___

KEY (CORRECT ANSWERS)

1. D	11. B	21. B	31. E	41. A
2. C	12. C	22. A	32. C	42. D
3. D	13. E	23. E	33. B	43. B
4. C	14. D	24. A	34. D	44. E
5. E	15. E	25. E	35. A	45. D
6. C	16. C	26. B	36. C	46. A
7. E	17. D	27. D	37. A	47. D
8. C	18. A	28. A	38. E	48. E
9. B	19. D	29. C	39. A	49. C
10. C	20. D	30. B	40. C	50. C

EXAMINATION SECTION

DIRECTIONS: Each question or incomplete statement is followed by several suggested answers or completions. Select the one that BEST answers the question or completes the statement. *PRINT THE LETTER OF THE CORRECT ANSWER IN THE SPACE AT THE RIGHT.*

1. Which combination of the following statements is FALSE?   1.___
      I. A stock certificate is evidence of a participation in ownership of a corporation.
     II. Par value of stock has no relationship to its worth.
    III. The par value of a share of stock is an indication of its market value.
     IV. No-par value stock is carried on the books of a corporation at an amount which is called the stated value.

   The CORRECT answer is:
      A. I, IV   B. I, II, IV   C. II, III
      D. I, II, III   E. III *only*

2. Which combination of the following statements is FALSE?   2.___
      I. All business must issue capital stock before commencing operations.
     II. Payment of dividends is required of all corporations.
    III. Dividends can only be paid from current earnings.
     IV. Annual dividends per share can never exceed annual earnings per share.

   The CORRECT answer is:
      A. I, II   B. I, II, III, IV   C. IV *only*
      D. I, II, IV   E. III *only*

3. Which combination of the following statements is TRUE?   3.___
      I. Guaranteed stocks are stocks guaranteed as to dividends by individuals or by a company or companies other than the one issuing the stock.
     II. When a corporation splits its stock or declares a stock dividend, the stockholders have a greater interest in the assets and earnings of the company.
    III. The rights of a holder of a voting trust certificate for common stock of a corporation are identical to those of an owner of common stock.
     IV. A preferred stock has prior claim over the common stock in a distribution of earnings of a corporation as specified in the charter of the corporation.

   The CORRECT answer is:
      A. I, II   B. I, II, III   C. I, IV
      D. I, II, III, IV E. II, III

4. Which combination of the following statements is TRUE?   4.__
   I. A preferred stock is a security senior to a bond of
      the same issuer.
   II. Preferred stock is so termed because of certain
       preferences that it commands over common stock.
   III. Cumulative preferred stock entitles the owner to
        receive passed or unpaid dividends for prior periods
        if earned and declared in subsequent periods.
   IV. Participating preferred stock gives the owner the
       right to participate with holders of common stock
       in earnings over and above the stipulated preferred
       stock dividend rate under certain conditions.

   The CORRECT answer is:
   A. I, IV   B. II, III, IV   C. I, III, IV
   D. IV *only*   E. III *only*

5. Which combination of the following statements is FALSE?   5.__
   I. A bond is an evidence of ownership of a corporation.
   II. A bondholder is a creditor of the corporation whose
       bonds he holds.
   III. A coupon bond is payable to the bearer at maturity
        and contains coupons which may be presented for
        payment on interest dates.
   IV. Certain registered bonds have the name of the owner
       written on the face of the bonds as well as in the
       books of the issuer.

   The CORRECT answer is:
   A. I, II   B. I, III   C. I *only*
   D. I, III, IV   E. II, III, IV

6. Which combination of the following statements is TRUE?   6.__
   I. A mortgage bond is an evidence of indebtedness which
      is secured by a mortgage or other lien on some under-
      lying real property of a corporation.
   II. General mortgage bonds are frequently backed by a
       blanket mortgage (but not necessarily a first mort-
       gage) on all of the corporation's fixed capital assets.
   III. Open-end mortgage bonds permit a corporation to bor-
        row additional money under the same mortgage, but
        almost always provide against a reduction in the
        value of property per dollar of debt by stipulating
        that additional property must be included under the
        mortgage as the amount of the mortgage is increased.
   IV. Closed-end mortgage bonds specify that the original
       issue has priority on claims and may not be issued
       beyond the specified amount of the issue.

   The CORRECT answer is:
   A. I, II   B. I, II, III   C. I, II, III, IV
   D. II, III   E. II, III, IV

7. Which combination of the following statements is FALSE?   7.___
    I. A debenture is an evidence of indebtedness which is not secured by a lien on any specific property.
    II. A debenture is the printed material on the face of a bond, which sets forth the terms and conditions of the bond issue and eventual repayment.
    III. Debentures have no specific collateral behind them. They are simply promises to pay and are backed by the general credit and assets of the corporation by which they are issued.
    IV. Debentures differ from stock in that they promise to repay the principal on a specified date, with regular interest.

The CORRECT answer is:
    A. I, II, III   B. II *only*   C. III *only*
    D. I, IV   E. IV *only*

8. Which combination of the following statements is TRUE?   8.___
    I. Convertible bonds can be converted usually into stock at a specified price or ratio.
    II. Convertible bonds cannot be secured by mortgage or collateral.
    III. A convertible debenture is a security representing an evidence of indebtedness which, at the option of the holder and subject to stated conditions, may be converted into some other security of a corporation.
    IV. Most often convertible bonds are debentures rather than mortgage or collateral trust bonds.

The CORRECT answer is:
    A. I, III, IV   B. II, IV   C. I, II, III
    D. II, III, IV   E. I *only*

9. Which combination of the following statements is FALSE?   9.___
    I. Guaranteed bonds are guaranteed by others than the corporation issuing the bonds.
    II. Guarantees on a guaranteed bond may extend to interest, principal, or both.
    III. An income bond is an evidence of indebtedness, the interest on which is normally paid only out of available income of the corporation.
    IV. Income or adjustment bonds may require the issuer to pay specified interest rates only if earned. They may be cumulative or noncumulative.

The CORRECT answer is:
    A. I *only*   B. I, II
    C. I, III, IV   D. I, II, III, IV
    E. None of the above

10. Which combination of the following statements is TRUE?   10.__
    I. *Municipals* is a term applied to the obligations of
       states, local governments, and authorities.
    II. Securities issued by towns, cities, states, and the
        Federal Government are all termed *municipals*.
    III. The income that municipal bonds provide is exempt
         from Federal income taxes.
    IV. Most states give preferential tax treatment to their
        own municipal bonds.

    The CORRECT answer is:
    A. I, II, III   B. II, III, IV
    C. I, II, III   D. I, III, IV
    E. None of the above

11. Which combination of the following statements is FALSE?   11.__
    I. A proxy is a power of attorney granted by a stock-
       holder authorizing another person to vote his stock.
    II. Warrants usually represent privileges to buy stock
        under specified conditions.
    III. Rights or subscription rights represent privileges
         to buy securities at specified prices.
    IV. Voting trust certificates are issued for stock
        deposited under a voting trust where it is deemed
        desirable to grant control of a corporation to a
        group of individuals for a time, or under certain
        conditions.

    The CORRECT answer is:
    A. I *only*   B. I, II, III
    C. I, II, III, IV   D. I, IV
    E. None of the above

12. Which combination of the following statements is FALSE?   12.__
    I. Securities listed on a national securities exchange
       may not be traded over-the-counter.
    II. Securities not traded on a securities exchange are
        said to be traded over-the-counter.
    III. A broker is one who buys and sells securities for
         the account and risk of others and may receive a
         commission for his services.
    IV. A broker is engaged in the business of buying and
        selling securities only for his own account and risk.

    The CORRECT answer is:
    A. I, II   B. I, IV
    C. I, II, III, IV   D. I, II, IV
    E. None of the above

13. Which combination of the following statements is TRUE?   13.__
    I. A broker/dealer registered with the Securities and
       Exchange Commission and engaged in the investment
       banking and securities business may buy and sell
       securities for his own account and risk.

II. A broker/dealer registered with the Securities and
Exchange Commission and engaged in the investment
banking and securities business may, as agent,
purchase and sell securities for the account and risk
of others.

III. A person acts *as agent* when he executes orders for
the account and risk of others, whether or not he
charges a commission for his services.

IV. The terms *broker* and *agent* mean the same thing.

The CORRECT answer is:
A. I, II, IV   B. I, II
C. II, IV   D. I, II, III, IV
E. None of the above

14. Which combination of the following statements is FALSE?   14.___

I. An agent or broker who is acting for both the buyer
and the seller in the purchase and sale of securities
need not disclose his commissions to the parties on
both sides of the transactions.

II. An agent or a broker must disclose to his customer
commissions charged in connection with the purchase
or sale of securities.

III. A dealer may sell securities to a customer even
though he does not own the securities at the time of
the sale.

IV. Typically, a dealer buys for his own account and sells
to a customer from his own inventory.

The CORRECT answer is:
A. I *only*   B. I, II
C. III, IV   D. I, II, III, IV
E. None of the above

15. Which combination of the following statements is TRUE?   15.___

I. An investment banker is frequently an underwriter -
one who usually contracts to buy securities from
an issuer which he intends to resell.

II. An investment banker may join with other underwriters
in buying and selling.

III. In an underwriting, the investment banking group
usually buys the securities from the issuing corporation at a specific price with the purpose of reselling
the securities at an offering price which includes
the group's compensation.

IV. Investment bankers may distribute very large blocks
of stocks or bonds - perhaps owned by an estate.

The CORRECT answer is:
A. I, II   B. I, III, IV
C. I, II, III   D. All of the above
E. None of the above

16. Which combination of the following statements is TRUE?   16.__
    I. A national securities exchange is a membership
       institution which provides facilities for its members
       to execute transactions in securities traded thereon
       for their own account or for the account and risk of
       others.
    II. National securities exchanges often permit non-members
       to go on the floor of the exchange to execute trans-
       actions in person for their own account and risk.
    III. A registered national securities association is an
       organization created pursuant to the provisions of
       Federal law to adopt, administer, and enforce rules
       of fair practice in connection with transactions in
       securities which do not take place on the floor of
       any registered securities exchange.
    IV. Securities exchanges or stock exchanges neither buy
       nor sell securities.

    The CORRECT answer is:
       A. I, II   B. I, III
       C. I, III, IV   D. All of the above
       E. None of the above

17. Which combination of the following statements is FALSE?   17.__
    I. The process whereby an original offering of securities
       is sold to investors is called a *primary distribution*.
    II. A *secondary distribution* is the term usually applied
       to the process whereby a large block of securities
       which has already been issued is sold and redistri-
       buted to others.
    III. A *secondary distribution* is handled off the NYSE by
       a securities firm or group of firms and the shares
       are usually offered at a fixed price which is related
       to the current market price of the stock.
    IV. *Private placement* generally means the direct sale of
       an issue of securities to institutional investors.

    The CORRECT answer is:
       A. I, II   B. I, IV
       C. I, II, IV   D. I, II, III, IV
       E. None of the above

18. Which combination of the following statements is FALSE?   18.__
    I. The over-the-counter market is primarily a *negotiated*
       market. Buyers and sellers negotiate prices on the
       most favorable basis they think they can achieve.
    II. One characteristic of a stock exchange is that it is
       an *auction* market in which the buyer making the
       highest bid buys and the seller with the lowest offer
       sells.
    III. One characteristic of over-the-counter trading is
       that it takes place in a negotiated market, as opposed
       to the auction market on an exchange.
    IV. An over-the-counter dealer who has orders to buy or
       sell listed securities must execute such orders on
       the exchange on which securities are listed.

The CORRECT answer is:
A. I, II
B. II, III
C. IV *only*
D. All of the above
E. None of the above

19. Which combination of the following statements is TRUE? 19.___
   I. A security which is listed on a registered securities exchange may also be traded over-the-counter.
   II. Securities traded over-the-counter must meet certain minimum requirements in order to be approved for quoting by the National Quotations Committee of the National Association of Securities Dealers, Inc.
   III. Published over-the-counter securities quotations are *bid and asked* prices which do not represent actual transactions. They are intended as a guide to the approximate range within which these securities could have been sold (indicated by *bids*) or bought (indicated by the *asked* prices) at the time the prices were given.
   IV. Prices published in the newspapers under the sponsorship of the National Association of Securities Dealers, Inc., represent ranges within which members of the public might reasonably expect to be able to buy or sell at the time the prices were furnished.

   The CORRECT answer is:
   A. I, IV
   B. I, II, IV
   C. I, II, III
   D. I, II, III, IV
   E. None of the above

20. Mrs. Adler had a gain of $36,000. Four business days 20.___
   before the end of the year, she made trades resulting in
   a gain of $8,000 and a loss of $7,000.
   Her taxable position is a gain of _____ and a loss of
   _____.
   A. $44,000; $7,000
   B. $36,000; $7,000
   C. $29,000; $7,000
   D. $28,000; $7,000
   E. None of the above

21. Which combination of the following statements is FALSE? 21.___
   I. As to most open-end investment company shares, net asset value per share and the *bid* price in the newspapers are the same.
   II. The offering price of an open-end investment company share is the net asset value per share, plus the sales charge, and is the same as the *asked* price in the newspapers.
   III. Dollar cost averaging means investing equal amounts of money at regular intervals regardless of price levels.
   IV. Dollar cost averaging assures against loss in value in declining markets.

   The CORRECT answer is:
   A. I, IV
   B. II, IV
   C. IV *only*
   D. III, IV
   E. None of the above

22. Which combination of the following statements is FALSE?   22.___
    I. Unless a trader specifies to the contrary, the prices
       he quotes for a particular security are firm at the
       moment for amounts equivalent to the usual trading
       units for such security.
   II. The price which will be paid for a given security is
       called a *bid*.
  III. The actual number of shares or bonds represented in
       a bid or offering, which comprises a given market
       quotation, is called the *size* of the offering or bid.
   IV. The difference between the bid and asked prices is
       known as the spread.

The CORRECT answer is:
    A. I *only*   B. IV *only*
    C. I, II, III   D. I, II, III, IV
    E. None of the above

23. Which combination of the following statements is TRUE?   23.___
    I. The term *BW* means beware.
   II. The term *Bid Wanted* means a security is being
       offered for sale and prospective buyers are requested
       to submit a bid for it.
  III. The term *Offering Wanted* or *OW* means the security
       referred to is being sought for purchase and anyone
       wishing to sell is requested to submit an offering.
   IV. The term *GTC* means that the order remains in force
       but must be confirmed at least every six months on
       the last business day of April and of October.

The CORRECT answer is:
    A. I, II, III   B. II, III
    C. II, III, IV   D. III, IV
    E. None of the above

24. Which combination of the following statements is TRUE?   24.___
    I. A *firm offer* is a valid offer to sell a specified
       amount of a security at a definite price, whether
       for a brief moment only or for a specified period
       of time.
   II. *Offered firm* means that the seller has made an
       offering which is good for the period of time speci-
       fied by the seller or until rejected.
  III. *Firm bids* or *firm offers* are prices at which a
       dealer is committed to buy or sell securities.
   IV. A *firm bid* is a valid offer to buy a specified amount
       of a security at a definite price, whether for a
       brief moment only or for a specified period of time.

The CORRECT answer is:
    A. I, IV   B. I, II, III, IV
    C. IV *only*   D. II, III
    E. None of the above

25. Which combination of the following statement is TRUE? 25.___
    I. Unless the number of shares of a security named in a *firm bid* or *offer* is specified, it is understood to be the usual trading unit of the security - generally 100 shares.
   II. A trade is consummated by the statement *we buy* or *we sell* and by the response *we confirm*.
  III. *Actual market* is the price at which a given security may be bought or sold.
   IV. Anyone supplying a quotation as an *actual market* is under an obligation to make it good immediately to the extent of actually buying or selling an amount equal to the usual *size* of the market in that security, generally 100 shares or 5 bonds, unless he has specified a smaller or larger amount when making his *actual market*.

The CORRECT answer is:
    A. I, II, III, IV   B. II, III, IV
    C. II, III   D. III, IV
    E. None of the above

26. Which combination of the following statements is FALSE? 26.___
    I. *Firm* market prices are those at which a security can be bought or sold.
   II. Anyone claiming to have a *firm market* in a security is expected to be ready and obligated to buy or sell at the prices quoted in amounts equivalent to what is commonly understood to be the trading unit in that security, unless he designates a smaller or larger amount as his *firm market*.
  III. When a customer inquires how a security is quoted, it is sufficient if you tell him how your firm is offering that security.
   IV. A *quotation* at all times includes both sides of the market - even though one side may be non-existent as, for instance, *offered @ 30, no bid* or *30 bid, none offered*.

The CORRECT answer is:
    A. I, II, III   B. III *only*
    C. I, II   D. IV *only*
    E. All of the above

27. Which combination of the following statements is FALSE? 27.___
    I. A *work-out* market represents an indication of prices at which it is believed a security can be bought or sold within a reasonable length of time.
   II. A dealer is said to *maintain* a market in a security when he is known to be willing at all times to buy or sell that security.
  III. A *market order* is an order to buy or sell at the best obtainable price prevailing in the market when the order is entered.
   IV. An *open order* is an order entered at a specific price and is good until cancelled.

The CORRECT answer is:
A. All of the above   B. II, III
C. III, IV   D. I *only*
E. None of the above

28. Which combination of the following statements is TRUE?   28.__
    I. The term *dividend on* signifies that the buyer is entitled to the dividend declared on a security.
    II. *Ex-dividend* signifies that the buyer is entitled to the dividend declared on a security.
    III. On and after the *ex-dividend* date, the buyer is entitled, unless otherwise agreed, to a dividend which has been declared.
    IV. On stock of an open-end investment company, the ex-dividend date is the date designated by the issuer or its principal underwriter.

    The CORRECT answer is:
    A. I, IV   B. I, II, III, IV
    C. II, IV   D. I, III, IV
    E. None of the above

29. Which combination of the following statements is FALSE?   29.__
    I. The term *ex-interest* indicates that the buyer is not to receive the interest payment which is about to be paid on the security.
    II. A security which sells *without accrued interest*, generally an income or defaulted bond, is said to trade *flat*.
    III. If a security is traded *ex-rights*, the rights referred to are not to accompany the security.
    IV. *Cash* trades are transactions requiring delivery of the securities after the fifth day of sale.

    The CORRECT answer is:
    A. I, III, IV   B. II, III, IV
    C. III, IV   D. IV *only*
    E. None of the above

30. Which combination of the following statements is FALSE?   30.__
    I. When a bond is traded *flat*, only the dollar price is figured in settling the contract, no allowance being made for any accrued interest.
    II. Most corporation bonds trade *flat*.
    III. Most preferred stocks trade *and dividend*.
    IV. United States Government bonds trade *and interest*.

    The CORRECT answer is:
    A. I, II   B. II, III   C. III, IV
    D. I, IV   E. All of the above

31. Which combination of the following statements is TRUE?   31.___
    I. When it is known at the time of sale that securities cannot be delivered on the date prescribed for a *regular way* transaction, the seller must notify the purchaser after execution that it will be for *delayed delivery*.
    II. A trading unit is the customary number of shares or bonds required for any single purchase or sale of a particular security.
    III. A balance sheet of a business is intended to portray the financial position of that business as of a certain date by listing the items owned, items owed, and the equity of the owners.
    IV. Capitalization is the amount of funds invested in the business through issuance of common stock, preferred stock, and bonds.

    The CORRECT answer is:
       A. I, II, III   B. I, II   C. II, III, IV
       D. I, IV   E. All of the above

32. Which combination of the following statements is TRUE?   32.___
    I. The liquidating value of a share of stock is the theoretical amount per share which a stockholder could expect to receive if a corporation went out of existence by distributing all its assets to stockholders.
    II. The book value of a share of stock is the theoretical amount per share which a stockholder could expect to receive if a corporation went out of existence by distributing all its assets to stockholders.
    III. Book value is a good indication of the market value of a common stock on any specified date.
    IV. Unrealized securities profits are often termed *book* or *paper* profits.

    The CORRECT answer is:
       A. I, II, IV   B. I, II, III   C. II, IV
       D. I *only*   E. All of the above

33. Which combination of the following statements is FALSE?   33.___
    I. Interest rates are one of the least important factors affecting the price of high-grade bonds.
    II. Discount refers to the amount by which securities, particularly bonds, debentures, or preferred stock, sell below par or face value.
    III. Bonds selling at less than principal amount are said to be *at a discount*.
    IV. The prime rate, which is a posted rate, is the rate charged on loans to the largest business concerns.

    The CORRECT answer is:
       A. I, IV   B. II, IV
       C. III, IV   D. I *only*
       E. None of the above

34. Which combination of the following statements is FALSE? 34.__
    I. Bond premium refers to the amount such bonds are
       selling above par or face amount.
    II. Bond premium refers to the interest rate specified
        on the face of a bond.
    III. Bond prices and yields move conversely to each other;
         that is, rising yields mean lower prices and the
         converse.
    IV. Generally speaking, the larger the amount of a bond
        issue outstanding, the lesser its marketability.

    The CORRECT answer is:
      A. I, II   B. II, III, IV
      C. I *only*   D. I, II, IV
      E. None of the above

35. Which combination of the following statements is FALSE? 35.__
    I. The fact that open-end investment company shares are
       redeemable makes them extremely good vehicles for
       short-term investment.
    II. Investment companies normally invest in a large number
        of securities issues, and prices of investment com-
        pany shares are related to the market value of these
        portfolio securities.
    III. Prices of investment company shares move up and down
         in direct relation to stock market averages, which
         makes them particularly well-suited to the needs of a
         short-term speculator.
    IV. Open-end investment company shares are unique for many
        reasons, one being that prices of such shares are not
        related to supply and demand for the shares themselves,
        but rather to supply and demand for securities held
        in the investment company portfolio.

    The CORRECT answer is:
      A. I, II   B. II, III   C. I, III
      D. I, IV   E. I, II, III

36. Which combination of the following statements is TRUE? 36.__
    I. A balanced fund is an investment company whose stated
       policy is at all times to have some portion of its
       invested assets in bonds and preferred stocks, as
       well as in common stocks.
    II. A growth investment company is one whose stated
        objective is to seek short-term growth of capital by
        investing in the securities of companies which plow
        back a substantial part of earnings for expansion,
        research, or development purposes.
    III. A specialty or industry investment company is one
         which invests in the securities of companies in a
         single industry or in allied industries.
    IV. A unit investment trust is one which issues redeemable
        securities, each of which represents an undivided
        interest in a unit of a specified security.

The CORRECT answer is:
A. I, II, III   B. II, III
C. I, III, IV   D. All of the above
E. None of the above

37. Which combination of the following statements is FALSE?   37.___
   I. The term *discount*, as applied to closed-end investment company securities, means the amount the securities are selling above asset value.
  II. The term *premium*, as applied to closed-end investment company securities, means the amount the securities are selling below asset value.
 III. Net unrealized appreciation shown in an investment company's financial statement is the difference between cost and market value of securities held in the portfolio.
  IV. Net unrealized appreciation of an investment company, under some circumstances, could change to net unrealized loss without a purchase or sale of the underlying portfolio securities by the investment company management.

The CORRECT answer is:
A. III, IV   B. I, II, IV
C. I, II   D. II, III, IV
E. All of the above

38. In a Limited Partnership or DPP, which of the following   38.___
constitutes the powers, obligations, and limitation of the General Partner(s)?
   I. Ability to bind the partnership
  II. Exclusive right to manage the business
 III. Right to inspect the books and records
  IV. Admittance of Limited Partners

The CORRECT answer is:
A. I, II, IV   B. II, V
C. IV *only*   D. I, III
E. I, II, III, IV

39. Which combination of the following statements is FALSE?   39.___
   I. Securities which are referred to as *Blue Chips* are those which are qualified under *Blue Sky* laws of some states.
  II. The Dow-Jones averages are weighted averages of all securities listed on the New York Stock Exchange.
 III. A *Blue Chip* stock will pay dividends in both good times and bad.
  IV. Registration of securities under the Securities Act of 1933 automatically exempts a security from state registration requirements.

The CORRECT answer is:
A. I, II   B. III *only*
C. I, II, IV   D. III, IV
E. None of the above

40. Which of the following statements is FALSE?   40.__
    I. An offering circular generally must be used in connec-
       tion with sales of securities issued in amounts of
       $300,000 or less and qualified under Regulation A of
       the Securities and Exchange Commission.
    II. A *Red Herring* prospectus is one that is complete
        except for amendments as to price and any additional
        required information. It may be used to acquaint
        potential investors with essential facts in order to
        obtain indications of interest prior to the effective
        date of a registration statement.
    III. In the case of a new issue of stock of a nationally
         known company, where a registration statement has
         been filed but has not become effective, you may con-
         firm a sale of stock to a customer, provided he has
         seen a copy of the preliminary prospectus.
    IV. Every written communication soliciting an order of
        open-end investment company shares must be accompanied
        or preceded by a prospectus.

    The CORRECT answer is:
       A. I, II   B. III, IV
       C. III *only*   D. IV *only*
       E. None of the above

41. Which of the following statements is FALSE?   41.__
    I. The Securities Act of 1933 provides penalties of
       fine or imprisonment or both for false and misleading
       statements (or omissions) of a material nature con-
       tained in a registration statement or made in connec-
       tion with the sale of a security.
    II. The Securities and Exchange Commission approves
        securities registered with it and offered for sale
        under the Securities Act of 1933.
    III. The Securities and Exchange Commission guarantees the
         accuracy of the disclosures made in a prospectus or
         registration statement and passes upon the merits of
         a particular security as to which a registration
         statement is currently on file.
    IV. Offerings of securities pursuant to the provisions of
        Regulation A of the SEC (those amounting to $300,000
        or less) are subject to the Rules of Fair Practice of
        the National Association of Securities Dealers, Inc.

    The CORRECT answer is:
       A. I, II   B. II, III
       C. III, IV   D. I, II, III
       E. None of the above

42. Which combination of the following statements is TRUE? 42.__
    I. The Securities and Exchange Commission has prescribed
       no rules with respect to the maintenance of books,
       records, and accounts by registered brokers and
       dealers.

II. The Securities and Exchange Commission has prescribed rules governing the capital position of registered brokers and dealers, with particular reference to the ratio of the dealers' net aggregate indebtedness to the capital position.

III. A *regulated* investment company is not required to make provision for Federal income taxes on net income or capital gains that are paid out to shareholders or unrealized net appreciation of investments.

IV. Registration or licensing as a salesman in the state in which you conduct your principal activities automatically permits you to make sales in other states where registration is required.

The CORRECT answer is:
A. I, II
B. II, III
C. III, IV
D. I, II, III
E. None of the above

43. Which combination of the following statements is FALSE? 43.___

I. Any company which invests in securities is an investment company.

II. Open-end investment companies are often referred to as mutual funds.

III. An open-end investment company is an investment company whose shares normally are redeemable at current net asset value on demand of the shareholder.

IV. A closed-end investment company is an investment company which has a fixed number of shares of stock outstanding. Its shares are traded in the open market by broker/dealers, are often listed on securities exchanges, and sell at varying relationships to asset value.

The CORRECT answer is:
A. I *only*
B. III *only*
C. I, III
D. II, IV
E. None of the above

44. Which combination of the following statements is TRUE? 44.___

I. Closed-end investment companies continuously offer their securities to public investors.

II. The major difference between an open-end and closed-end investment company is that the former continuously offers and redeems its shares.

III. In principal transactions between dealers and customers in shares of open-end investment companies, the current public offering price must, by law, be maintained.

IV. Net asset value per share of an investment company equals the total net assets of the company (at the then current market value), divided by the number of shares outstanding at the same time.

The CORRECT answer is:
A. I, II
B. I, II, III
C. II, III, IV
D. I, II, IV
E. All of the above

45. Which combination of the following statements is FALSE?   45.__
I. The stock of a closed-end investment company must be redeemed by the issuer on any business day.
II. The holder of shares of a closed-end investment company may dispose of them only by turning them back to the issuer for redemption.
III. An investment company contractual plan holder can terminate his plan at any time, although in doing so, he may incur a penalty, depending upon the length of time he has participated in the plan.
IV. Decisions of management of investment companies are regulated by the SEC.

The CORRECT answer is:
A. I, II, III
B. II, III, IV
C. I, II, IV
D. II, IV
E. III *only*

46. Which combination of the following statements is FALSE?   46.__
I. In order to qualify as a *regulated* investment company under the Federal tax laws, an investment company must, among other things, distribute at least 97% of its investment income.
II. The reinvestment of capital gains distributions from an investment company (as distinguished from taking them in cash) avoids the capital gains tax.
III. An investor who receives a capital gains distribution from an investment company may regard it as *long-term* only if he has owned the shares for at least six months.
IV. Taking dividends in the shares of investment companies in lieu of cash, in most instances, saves a stockholder from paying income taxes on such dividends.

The CORRECT answer is:
A. I, II, III
B. II, III
C. II, III, IV
D. I, II, IV
E. All of the above

47. Which of the following statements is(are) TRUE?   47.__
I. The Standard & Poor 500 Index is composed of stocks from banks, industrials, transportation, and utilities.
II. The NYSE index measures the price change of unregistered listed securities.
III. The NASDAQ index includes a composit index as well as industrial, insurance, and bank stock issues.

The CORRECT answer is:
A. I *only*
B. III *only*
C. I, II
D. II, III
E. I, III

48. Which combination of the following statements is FALSE?   48.___
    I. Regulation T is a regulation adopted by the Board of
       Governors of the Federal Reserve System under the
       Securities Exchange Act of 1934, as amended, and
       relates to the extension of credit to customers by
       brokers and dealers doing business through the
       medium of a member of a national securities exchange.
    II. The *Cash Account* described in Regulation T is one in
        which customer transactions are effected with the
        understanding that they will be settled promptly.
    III. Regulation T states that on purchases for cash, if
         full payment is not made within 7 full business days
         of the trade date, the broker/dealer shall cancel or
         otherwise liquidate the transaction, unless an
         extension of time for payment for good cause is
         granted.
    IV. The Association has the authority, for good cause,
        to extend the time within which payment for securities
        purchased in any *special cash account* shall be made.

    The CORRECT answer is:
      A. I, II   B. II, III
      C. III, IV   D. IV *only*
      E. None of the above

49. Which combination of the following statements is FALSE?   49.___
    I. The buyer for a large life insurance company to whom
       you have offered a block of bonds which your firm
       owns, tells you on December 17th that his company
       has *closed* its books on new investments for the
       balance of the year, but he will buy the securities
       you have offered if your firm will deliver them
       against payment on January 2nd, in the New Year.
       There is no reason why you cannot sell him the bonds
       under these conditions.
    II. Extensions of time for payment under Regulation T may
        be secured from a committee of the Association or from
        any registered national securities exchange.
    III. A broker/dealer may carry a regular margin account
         for a customer if the account contains only securities
         not listed on a national securities exchange.
    IV. When a customer owes a broker/dealer less than $100
        in connection with a purchase transaction in a
        special cash account, the broker/dealer may disregard
        the provisions of Regulation T.

    The CORRECT answer is:
      A. I, II   B. I, III
      C. II, IV   D. III *only*
      E. None of the above

50. Which combination of the following statements is TRUE?   50.___
    I. The NASD administers a Statement of Policy issued
       by the Securities and Exchange Commission which
       states standards to govern sales literature used in
       the offering of open-end investment company shares
       and, where applicable, similar material relating to
       the securities of closed-end companies.
    II. In general, the material covered by the Statement of
        Policy involves all reports of issuers, brochures,
        sales letters, advertising by radio, television or
        newspaper, or any other material prepared by dealers,
        issuers, or underwriters with respect to investment
        company shares.
    III. Sales literature about investment company shares is
         not subject to the Statement of Policy if it is
         prepared by a dealer.
    IV. Dealers must file with the Association sales material
        prepared by sponsors of investment companies, as
        well as such items as are actually prepared in their
        own offices or for their use by outside agencies.

    The CORRECT answer is:
    A. I, II   B. I, III, IV
    C. I, II, IV   D. III, IV.
    E. None of the above

KEY (CORRECT ANSWERS)

1. E	11. E	21. C	31. C	41. B
2. B	12. B	22. E	32. A	42. B
3. C	13. D	23. C	33. D	43. A
4. B	14. A	24. B	34. B	44. C
5. C	15. D	25. A	35. C	45. C
6. C	16. C	26. B	36. C	46. C
7. B	17. E	27. E	37. C	47. D
8. A	18. C	28. A	38. A	48. E
9. E	19. D	29. D	39. C	49. B
10. D	20. A	30. D	40. C	50. A

EXAMINATION SECTION

TEST 1

DIRECTIONS: Each question or incomplete statement is followed by several suggested answers or completions. Select the one that BEST answers the question or completes the statement. *PRINT THE LETTER OF THE CORRECT ANSWER IN THE SPACE AT THE RIGHT.*

1. Gross income of an individual for Federal income tax purposes does NOT include
   A. interest credited to a bank savings account
   B. gain from the sale of sewer authority bonds
   C. back pay received as a result of job reinstatement
   D. interest received from State Dormitory Authority bonds

1.____

2. A cash-basis, calendar-year taxpayer purchased an annuity policy at a total cost of $20,000. Starting on January 1 of 1999, he began to receive annual payments of $1,500. His life expectancy as of that date was 16 years.
   The amount of annuity income to be included in his gross income for the taxable year 1999 is
   A. none   B. $250   C. $1,250   D. $1,500

2.____

3. The transactions related to a municipal police retirement system should be included in a(n)
   A. intra-governmental service fund
   B. trust fund
   C. general fund
   D. special revenue fund

3.____

4. The budget for a given cost during a given period was $100,000. The actual cost for the period was $90,000. Based upon these facts, one should say that the responsible manager has done a better than expected job in controlling the cost if the cost is
   A. variable and actual production equaled budgeted production
   B. a discretionary fixed cost and actual production equaled budgeted production
   C. variable and actual production was 90% of budgeted production
   D. variable and actual production was 80% of budgeted production

4.____

5. In the conduct of an audit, the *most practical* method by which an accountant can satisfy himself as to the physical existence of inventory is to
   A. be present and observe personally the audited firm's physical inventory being taken
   B. independently verify an adequate proportion of all inventory operations performed by the audited firm

5.____

C. mail confirmation requests to vendors of merchandise sold to the audited firm within the inventory year
D. review beforehand the adequacy of the audited firm's plan for inventory taking, and during the actual inventory-taking stages, verify that this plan is being followed

Questions 6-7.

DIRECTIONS: The following information applies to Questions 6 and 7.

For the month of March, the ABC Manufacturing Corporation's estimated factory overhead for an expected volume of 15,000 lbs. of a product was as follows:

	Amount	Overhead Rate Per Unit
Fixed Overhead	$3,000	$.20
Variable Overhead	$9,000	$.60

Actual volume was 10,000 lbs. and actual overhead expense was $7,700.

6. The Spending (Budget) Variance was
   A. $1,300 (Favorable)   B. $6,000 (Favorable)
   C. $7,700 (Favorable)   D. $9,000 (Favorable)

6.___

7. The Idle Capacity Variance was
   A. $300 (Favorable)   B. $1,000 (Unfavorable)
   C. $1,300 (Favorable)   D. $8,000 (Unfavorable)

7.___

Questions 8-11.

DIRECTIONS: Answer Questions 8 through 11 on the basis of the information given below.

A bookkeeper, who was not familiar with proper accounting procedures, prepared the following financial report for Largor Corporation as of December 31, 1939. In addition to the errors in presentation, additional data below was not considered in the preparation of the report. Restate this balance sheet in proper form, giving recognition to the additional data, so that you will be able to determine the required information to answer Questions 8 through 11.

LARGOR CORPORATION
December 31, 1999

Current Assets
Cash		$110,000	
Marketable Securities		53,000	
Accounts Receivable	$261,400		
Accounts Payable	125,000	136,400	
Inventories		274,000	
Prepaid Expenses		24,000	
Treasury Stock		20,000	
Cash Surrender Value of Officers' Life Insurance Policies		105,000	$722,400

Plant Assets
Equipment		350,000	
Building	200,000		
Reserve for Plant Expansion	75,000	125,000	
Land		47,500	522,500
TOTAL ASSETS			$1,244,900

Liabilities
Salaries Payable		16,500	
Cash Dividend Payable		50,000	
Stock Dividend Payable		70,000	
Bonds Payable	200,000		
Less Sinking Fund	90,000	110,000	
TOTAL LIABILITIES			$246,500

Stockholders' Equity
Paid In Capital
Common Stock		350,000	

Retained Earnings and Reserves
Reserve for Income Taxes	90,000		
Reserve for Doubtful Accounts	6,500		
Reserve for Treasury Stock	20,000		
Reserve for Depreciation - Equipment	70,000		
Reserve for Depreciation - Building	80,000		
Premium on Common Stock	15,000		
Retained Earnings	366,900	648,400	998,400
TOTAL LIABILITIES & EQUITY			$1,244,900

Additional Data
A. Bond Payable will mature eight (8) years from Balance Sheet date.
B. The Stock Dividend Payable was declared on December 31,1999.
C. The Reserve for Income Taxes represents the balance due on the estimated liability for taxes on income for the year ended December 31.
D. Advances from Customers at the Balance Sheet date totaled $13,600. This total is still credited against Accounts Receivable.
E. Prepaid Expenses include Unamortized Mortgage Costs of $15,000.
F. Marketable Securities were recorded at cost. Their market value at December 31, 1999 was $50,800.

8. After restatement of the balance sheet in proper form   8.____
   and giving recognition to the additional data, the Total
   Current Assets should be
      A. $597,400   B. $702,400   C. $712,300   D. $827,300

9. After restatement of the balance sheet in proper form and   9.____
   giving recognition to the additional data, the Total
   Current Liabilities should be
      A. $261,500   B. $281,500   C. $295,100   D. $370,100

10. After restatement of the balance sheet in proper form   10.____
    and giving recognition to the additional data, the net
    book value of plant and equipment should be
      A. $400,000   B. $447,500   C. $550,000   D. $597,500

11. After restatement of the balance sheet in proper form and   11.____
    giving recognition to the additional data, the Stockholders'
    Equity should be
      A. $320,000   B. $335,000   C. $764,700   D. $874,700

12. When preparing the financial statement, dividends in   12.____
    arrears on preferred stock should be treated as a
      A. contingent liability   B. deduction from capital
      C. parenthetical remark   D. valuation reserve

13. The IPC Corporation has an intangible asset which it   13.____
    values at $1,000,000 and has a life expectancy of 60 years.
    The *appropriate* span of write-off, as determined by good
    accounting practice, should be ____ years.
      A. 17   B. 34   C. 40   D. 60

14. The following information was used in costing inventory   14.____
    on October 31:
    October 1 - Beginning inventory - 800 units @ $1.20
             4 - Received   200 units @ $1.40
            16 - Issued   400 units
            24 - Received   200 units @ $1.60
            27 - Issued   500 units

    Using the LIFO method of inventory evaluation (end-of-
    month method), the total dollar value of the inventory at
    October 31 was
      A. $360   B. $460   C. $600   D. $1,200

15. If a $400,000 par value bond issue paying 8%, with   15.____
    interest dates of June 30 and December 31, is sold in
    November 1 for par plus accrued interest, the cash
    proceeds received by the issuer on November 1 should be
    approximately
      A. $405,000   B. $408,000   C. $411,000   D. $416,000

16. The TOTAL interest cost to the issuer of a bond issue   16.____
    sold for more than its face value is the periodic interest
    payment
      A. *plus* the discount amortization
      B. *plus* the premium amortization
      C. *minus* the discount amortization
      D. *minus* the premium amortization

17. If shareholders donate shares of stock back to the
company, such stock received by the company is *properly*
classified as
    A. Treasury stock
    B. Unissued stock
    C. Other assets – investment
    D. Current assets – investment

17.___

18. Assume the following transactions have occurred:
    1. 10,000 shares of capital stock of Omer Corp., par
       value $50, have been sold and issued on initial
       sale @ $55 per share during the month of June
    2. 2,000 shares of previously issued stock were purchased
       from shareholders during the month of September @
       $58 per share.

As of September 30, the stockholders' equity section TOTAL
should be
    A. $434,000   B. $450,000   C. $480,000   D. $550,000

18.___

19. Mr. Diak, a calendar-year taxpayer in the construction
business, agrees to construct a building for the Supermat
Corporation to cost a total of $500,000 and to require
about two years to complete. By December 31, 1985, he
has expended $150,000 in costs, and it was determined that
the building was 35% completed.
If Mr. Diak is reporting income under the completed contract
method, the amount of gross income he will report for 1985
is
    A. none   B. $25,000   C. $175,000   D. $350,000

19.___

20. When the Board of Directors of a firm uses the present-
value technique to aid in deciding whether or not to buy
a new plant asset, it needs to have information reflecting
    A. the cost of the new asset only
    B. the increased production from use of new asset only
    C. an estimated rate of return
    D. the book value of the asset

20.___

KEY (CORRECT ANSWERS)

1. D		11. D	
2. B		12. C	
3. B		13. C	
4. A		14. A	
5. D		15. C	
6. A		16. D	
7. B		17. A	
8. C		18. A	
9. C		19. A	
10. B		20. C	

TEST 2

Questions 1-3.

DIRECTIONS: The following information applies to Questions 1 through 3.

During your audit of the Avon Company, you find the following errors in the records of the company:

1. Incorrect exclusion from the final inventory of items costing $3,000 for which the purchase was not recorded.
2. Inclusion in the final inventory of goods costing $5,000, although a purchase was not recorded. The goods in question were being held on consignment from Reldrey Company.
3. Incorrect exclusion of $2,000 from the inventory count at the end of the period. The goods were in transit (F.O.B. shipping point); the invoice had been received and the purchase recorded.
4. Inclusion of items on the receiving dock that were being held for return to the vendor because of damage. In counting the goods in the receiving department, these items were incorrectly included. With respect to these goods, a purchase of $4,000 had been recorded.

The records (uncorrected) showed the following amounts:
1. Purchases, $170,000
2. Pretax income, $15,000
3. Accounts payable, $20,000; and
4. Inventory at the end of the period, $40,000.

1. The *corrected* inventory is
   A. $36,000   B. $42,000   C. $43,000   D. $44,000   1.___

2. The *corrected* income for the year is
   A. $12,000   B. $15,000   C. $17,000   D. $18,000   2.___

3. The *correct* accounts payable liabilities are
   A. $16,000   B. $17,000   C. $19,000   D. $23,000   3.___

4. An auditing procedure that is *most likely* to reveal the existence of a contingent liability is   4.___
   A. a review of vouchers paid during the month following the year end
   B. confirmation of accounts payable
   C. an inquiry directed to legal counsel
   D. confirmation of mortgage notes

Questions 5-6.

DIRECTIONS: The following information is to be used in answering Questions 5 and 6.

Mr. Zelev operates a business as a sole proprietor and uses the cash basis for reporting income for income tax purposes. IIis bank account during 1999 for the business shows receipts totaling $285,000 and cash payments totaling $240,000. Included in the cash payments were payments for three-year business insurance policies whose premiums totaled $1,575. It was determined that the expired premiums for this year were $475. Further examination of the accounts and discussion with Mr. Zelev revealed the fact that included in the receipts were the following items, as well as the proceeds received from customers:

$15,000 which Mr. Zelev took from his savings account and deposited in the business account.

$20,000 which Mr. Zelev received from the bank as a loan which will be repaid next year.

Included in the cash payments were $10,000 which Mr. Zelev took on a weekly basis from the business receipts to use for his personal expenses.

5. The amount of net income to be reported for income tax purposes for calendar year 1999 for Mr. Zelev is   5.___
      A. $21,100   B. $26,100   C. $31,100   D. $46,100

6. Assuming the same facts as those reported above, Mr. Zelev   6.___
    would be required to pay a self-employment tax for 1985 of
      A. $895.05   B. $1,208.70   C. $1,234.35   D. $1,666.90

7. For the year ended December 31, 1999, you are given the   7.___
    following information relative to the income and expense
    statements for the Sungam Manufacturers, Inc.:

Sales $1,000,000
    Sales Returns   95,000

Cost of Sales
Opening Inventories $200,000
Purchases During the Year   567,000
Direct Labor Costs   240,000
Factory Overhead   24,400
Inventories End of Year   235,000

On June 15, 1999, a fire destroyed the plant and all of the inventories then on hand. You are given the following information and asked to ascertain the amount of the estimated inventory loss.

Sales up to June 15 $545,000
Purchased to June 15   254,500
Direct Labor   233,000
Overhead   14,550
Salvaged Inventory   95,000

The *estimated* inventory loss is
    A. $95,000   B. $162,450   C. $189,450   D. $257,450

8. Losses and excessive costs with regard to inventory can occur in any one of several operating functions of an organization.
The operating function which bears the GREATEST responsibility for the failure to give proper consideration to transportation costs of material acquisitions is
    A. accounting   B. purchasing
    C. receiving   D. shipping

8.____

Questions 9-17.

DIRECTIONS: Questions 9 through 17 are to be answered on the basis of the information given below.

You are conducting an audit of the PAP Company, which has a contract to supply the municipal hospitals with specialty refrigerators on a cost-plus basis. The following information is available:

Materials purchased	$1,946,700
Inventories, January 1	
Materials	268,000
Finished Goods (100 units)	43,000
Direct Labor	2,125,800
Factory Overhead (40% variable)	764,000
Marketing Expenses (all fixed)	516,000
Administrative Expenses (all fixed)	461,000
Sales (12,400 units)	6,634,000
Inventories, March 31	
Materials	167,000
Finished Goods (200 units)	(omitted)
No Work In Process	

9. The *net income* for the period is
    A. $755,500   B. $1,237,500
    C. $1,732,500   D. $4,980,500

9.____

10. The *number* of units manufactured is
    A. 12,400   B. 12,500   C. 12,600   D. 12,700

10.____

11. The *unit cost* of refrigerators manufactured is *most nearly*
    A. $389.00   B. $395.00   C. $398.00   D. $400.00

11.____

12. The *total* variable costs are
    A. $305,600   B. $764,000
    C. $4,479,100   D. $4,937,500

12.____

13. The *total* fixed costs are
    A. $458,400   B. $1,435,400
    C. $1,471,800   D. $1,741,000

13.____

While you are conducting your audit, the PAP Company advises you that they have changed their inventory costing from FIFO to LIFO. You are interested in pursuing the matter further because this change will affect the cost of the refrigerators. An examination of material part 2-317 inventory card shows the following activity:

May 2 - Received 100 units @ $5.40 per unit
May 8 - Received 30 units @ $8.00 per unit
May 15 - Issued 50 units
May 22 - Received 120 units @ $9.00 per unit
May 29 - Issued 100 units

14. Using the FIFO method under a perpetual inventory control   14.___
    system, the *total* cost of the units issued in May is
       A. $690   B. $960   C. $1,590   D. $1,860

15. Using the FIFO method under a perpetual inventory control   15.___
    system, the *value* of the closing inventory is
       A. $780   B. $900   C. $1,080   D. $1,590

16. Using the LIFO method under a perpetual inventory control   16.___
    system, the *total* cost of the units issued in May is
       A. $1,248   B. $1,428   C. $1,720   D. $1,860

17. Using the LIFO method under a perpetual inventory control   17.___
    system, the *value* of the closing inventory is
       A. $612   B. $780   C. $1,512   D. $1,680

Questions 18-20.

DIRECTIONS: For Questions 18 through 20, consider that the EEF
             Corporation has a fully integrated cost accounting
             system.

18. Unit cost of manufacturing dresses was $7.00. Spoiled   18.___
    dresses numbered 400 with a sales value of $800. When
    it is not customary to have a Spoiled Work account, the
    most appropriate account to be credited is
       A. Work In Process   B. Cost of Sales
       C. Manufacturing Overhead D. Finished Goods

19. Overtime premium for factory workers (direct labor)   19.___
    totaled $400 for the payroll period. This was due to
    inadequate plant capacity. The account to be *debited* is
       A. Work In Process   B. Cost of Sales
       C. Manufacturing Overhead D. Finished Goods

20. A month-end physical inventory of stores shows a shortage   20.___
    of $175. The account to be *debited* to correct this
    shortage is
       A. Stores   B. Work In Process
       C. Cost of Sales   D. Manufacturing Overhead

KEY (CORRECT ANSWERS)

1.	A	11.	B
2.	A	12.	C
3.	C	13.	B
4.	C	14.	B
5.	A	15.	B
6.	D	16.	A
7.	B	17.	A
8.	B	18.	A
9.	A	19.	C
10.	B	20.	C

EXAMINATION SECTION

TEST 1

DIRECTIONS: Each question or incomplete statement is followed by several suggested answers or completions. Select the one that BEST answers the question or completes the statement. *PRINT THE LETTER OF THE CORRECT ANSWER IN THE SPACE AT THE RIGHT.*

1. Revenue from the parking lot operated by a hospital would NORMALLY be included in _____ revenue.
   A. patient service
   B. ancillary service
   C. other operating
   D. other nonoperating

1.___

2. The plant funds group of a not-for-profit private university includes which of the following subgroups?

	Investment in plant funds	Unexpended plant funds
A.	No	Yes
B.	No	No
C.	Yes	No
D.	Yes	Yes

2.___

3. The comprehensive annual financial report (CAFR) of a governmental unit should contain a combined statement of changes in financial position for

	Governmental funds	Account groups
A.	Yes	No
B.	Yes	Yes
C.	No	Yes
D.	No	No

3.___

4. How would customers' security deposits which cannot be spent for normal operating purposes be classified in the balance sheet of the enterprise fund of a governmental unit?

	Restricted asset	Liability	Fund equity
A.	Yes	No	Yes
B.	Yes	Yes	No
C.	Yes	Yes	Yes
D.	No	Yes	No

4.___

5. The TOTAL assets of the general long-term debt account group of a governmental unit consist of the amount
   A. available in debt service funds account plus the amount to be provided for retirement of general long-term debt account
   B. available in debt service funds account minus the amount to be provided for retirement of general long-term debt account
   C. available in debt service funds account only
   D. to be provided for retirement of general long-term debt account only

5.___

6. Interest on bonds issued by the special assessment fund   6.___
   of a governmental unit would be accounted for through the
   A. general fund
   B. debt service fund
   C. special assessment fund
   D. general long-term debt account group

7. Which of the following funds of a governmental unit   7.___
   integrates budgetary accounts into the accounting system?
   A. Enterprise   B. Internal service
   C. Special revenue   D. Nonexpendable trust

8. Which of the following accounts of a governmental unit   8.___
   is debited when supplies previously ordered are received?
   A. Appropriations control
   B. Encumbrances control
   C. Fund balance reserved for encumbrances
   D. Vouchers payable

9. When the budget of a governmental unit, for which the   9.___
   estimated revenues exceed the appropriations, is adopted
   and recorded in the general ledger at the beginning of
   the year, the budgetary fund balance account is _____
   at the beginning of the year and _____ at the end of the
   year.
   A. credited; no entry made   B. credited; debited
   C. debited; no entry made   D. debited; credited

10. Which of the following is an appropriate basis of   10.___
    accounting for a proprietary fund of a governmental unit?

	Cash basis	Modified accrual basis
A.	Yes	Yes
B.	Yes	No
C.	No	No
D.	No	Yes

11. Simple regression analysis involves the use of   11.___

	Dependent variables	Independent variables
A.	One	None
B.	One	One
C.	One	Two
D.	None	Two

12. If income tax considerations are ignored, how is depreci-   12.___
    ation expense used in the following capital budgeting
    techniques?

	Internal rate of return	Net present value
A.	Excluded	Excluded
B.	Excluded	Included
C.	Included	Excluded
D.	Included	Included

13. The contribution margin ratio ALWAYS increases when the   13.___
    A. variable costs as a percentage of net sales increase
    B. variable costs as a percentage of net sales decrease
    C. breakeven point increases
    D. breakeven point decreases

14. The invested capital-employed turnover rate would include   14.___
    A. sales in the denominator
    B. net income in the numerator
    C. invested capital in the denominator
    D. invested capital in the numerator

15. When a flexible budget is used, a decrease in production   15.___
    levels within a relevant range would
    A. decrease variable cost per unit
    B. decrease total costs
    C. increase total fixed costs
    D. increase variable cost per unit

16. In an income statement prepared as an internal report   16.___
    using the variable costing method, fixed factory overhead
    would
    A. not be used
    B. be used in the computation of operating income but
       not in the computation of the contribution margin
    C. be used in the computation of the contribution margin
    D. be treated the same as variable factory overhead

17. Byproducts could have which of the following characteris-   17.___
    tics?

	Zero costs beyond split-off	Additional costs beyond split-off
A.	No	No
B.	No	Yes
C.	Yes	Yes
D.	Yes	No

18. Under the two-variance method for analyzing factory over-   18.___
    head, the difference between the actual factory overhead
    and the budget allowance based on standard hours allowed
    is the _____ variance.
    A. net overhead   B. efficiency
    C. volume   D. controllable (budget)

19. Costs are accumulated by responsibility center for   19.___
    control purposes when using

	Job order costing	Process costing
A.	Yes	Yes
B.	Yes	No
C.	No	No
D.	No	Yes

20. Prime cost and conversion cost share what common element   20.___
    of total cost?
    A. Direct labor   B. Direct materials
    C. Variable overhead   D. Fixed overhead

21. Personal financial statements consist of a statement of   21.___
    financial condition and USUALLY a(n)

	Income statement	Statement of changes in net worth
A.	No	No
B.	No	Yes
C.	Yes	Yes
D.	Yes	No

22. How are each of the following used in the calculation   22.___
    of the receivable turnover?

	Cash sales	Credit sales
A.	Not used	Numerator
B.	Not used	Denominator
C.	Numerator	Numerator
D.	Denominator	Denominator

23. If the payment of compensation is probable, the amount   23.___
    can be reasonably estimated, and the obligation relates
    to rights that vest, employees' compensation for future
    absences should be
    A. accrued if attributable to employees' services
       already rendered
    B. accrued if attributable to employees' services not
       already rendered
    C. accrued if attributable to employees' services
       whether already rendered or not
    D. recognized when paid

24. In financial reporting for segments of a business enter-   24.___
    prise, the operating profit or loss of a manufacturing
    segment should include

	Interest expense	Income taxes
A.	Yes	Yes
B.	Yes	No
C.	No	Yes
D.	No	No

25. Pro forma effects on net income and earnings per share   25.___
    of retroactive application would USUALLY be reported on
    the face of the income statement for a

	Change in accounting entity	Change in accounting estimate
A.	Yes	Yes
B.	Yes	No
C.	No	No
D.	No	Yes

26. For interim financial reporting, which of the following   26.___
    may be accrued or deferred to provide an appropriate cost
    in each period?

	Property taxes	Rent
A.	No	No
B.	No	Yes
C.	Yes	Yes
D.	Yes	No

27. In a business combination, costs of registering equity   27.___
    securities are a reduction of the otherwise determinable
    fair value of the securities for a

	Pooling of interests	Purchase
A.	No	No
B.	No	Yes
C.	Yes	Yes
D.	Yes	No

28. Company A and Company B exchanged non-monetary assets   28.___
    with monetary consideration involved. The exchange did
    not culminate an earning process for either Company A
    or Company B.
    The recipient of the monetary consideration has
    A. realized gain on the exchange to the extent of the
       monetary consideration received
    B. realized gain on the exchange to the extent that the
       amount of the monetary consideration received exceeds
       the recorded amount of the asset surrendered
    C. realized gain on the exchange to the extent that
       the amount of the monetary consideration received
       exceeds a proportionate share of the recorded amount
       of the asset surrendered
    D. no realized gain on the exchange

29. In determining earnings per share in a complex capital   29.___
    structure, which of the following is a common stock
    equivalent?

	Nonconvertible preferred stock	Stock option
A.	Yes	No
B.	Yes	Yes
C.	No	Yes
D.	No	No

30. When a segment of a business has been discontinued during   30.___
    the year, the loss on disposal should
    A. included operating losses of the current period up to
       the measurement date
    B. include operating losses during the phase-out period
    C. exclude employee relocation costs associated with
       the decision to dispose
    D. exclude severance pay associated with the decision
       to dispose

KEY (CORRECT ANSWERS)

1. C	6. C	11. B	16. B	21. B	26. C
2. D	7. C	12. A	17. C	22. A	27. B
3. D	8. C	13. B	18. D	23. A	28. C
4. B	9. B	14. C	19. A	24. D	29. C
5. A	10. C	15. B	20. A	25. C	30. B

TEST 2

1. A loss on the sale of a long-term investment should be presented in a statement of changes in financial position as a(n)
   A. addition to income from continuing operations
   B. deduction from income from continuing operations
   C. source and a use of funds
   D. use of funds

   1.___

2. A company declared a property dividend to be paid by distributing inventory. The fair value of the inventory is the same as its carrying value.
   In a statement of changes in financial position prepared on a working capital basis, this transaction should be presented as a(n)
   A. addition to income from continuing operations
   B. deduction from income from continuing operations
   C. source and a use of funds
   D. use of funds

   2.___

3. Timing differences affect

	Interperiod income tax allocation	Intraperiod income tax allocation
A.	Yes	No
B.	Yes	Yes
C.	No	Yes
D.	No	No

   3.___

4. Which of the following utilizes the straight-line depreciation method?

	Composite depreciation	Group depreciation
A.	Yes	Yes
B.	Yes	No
C.	No	Yes
D.	No	No

   4.___

5. A company issued rights to its existing shareholders to purchase shares of common stock.
   When the rights are exercised, additional paid-in capital would be credited if the purchase price
   A. exceeded the par value
   B. was the same as the par value
   C. was the same as the par value but less than the market value at the date of exercise
   D. was less than the par value

   5.___

6. A company uses the percentage-of-completion method to   6.___
   account for a four-year construction contract.
   Which of the following would be used in the calculation
   of the income recognized in the first year?

	Progress billings	Collections on progress billings
A.	No	No
B.	No	Yes
C.	Yes	No
D.	Yes	Yes

7. A sale of goods, denominated in a currency other than   7.___
   the entity's functional currency, resulted in a receivable
   that was fixed in terms of the amount of foreign currency
   that would be received. Exchange rates between the
   functional currency and the currency in which the transaction was denominated changed.
   The resulting gain should be included as a
       A. translation gain reported as a separate component
          of stockholders' equity
       B. translation gain reported as a component of income
          from continuing operations
       C. transaction gain reported as a separate component of
          stockholders' equity
       D. transaction gain reported as a component of income
          from continuing operations

8. Treasury stock was acquired for cash at a price in excess   8.___
   of its par value. The treasury stock was subsequently
   sold for cash at a price in excess of its acquisition
   price.
   Assuming that the cost method of accounting for treasury
   stock transactions is used, what is the effect on total
   stockholders' equity?

	Purchase of treasury stock	Sale of treasury stock
A.	Increase	Decrease
B.	Decrease	No effect
C.	Decrease	Increase
D.	No effect	No effect

9. How would total stockholders' equity be affected by the   9.___
   declaration of each of the following?

	Stock dividend	Stock split
A.	No effect	Increase
B.	Decrease	Decrease
C.	Decrease	No effect
D.	No effect	No effect

10. The correction of an error in the financial statements   10.___
    of a prior period should be reflected, net of applicable
    income taxes, in the current
        A. income statement after income from contining opera-
           tions and before extraordinary items
        B. income statement after income from continuing opera-
           tions and after extraordinary items

C. retained earnings statement as an adjustment of the opening balance

D. retained earnings statement after net income but before dividends

11. The issuance of shares of preferred stock to shareholders   11.___
    A. increases preferred stock outstanding
    B. has no effect on preferred stock outstanding
    C. increases preferred stock authorized
    D. decreases preferred stock authorized

12. Outstanding bonds payable are converted into common   12.___
    stock.
    Under either the book value or market value method, the
    same amount would be debited to

	Bonds payable	Premium on bonds payable
A.	No	No
B.	No	Yes
C.	Yes	No
D.	Yes	Yes

13. How would the carrying value of a bond payable be   13.___
    affected by amortization of each of the following?

	Discount	Premium
A.	No effect	No effect
B.	Increase	No effect
C.	Increase	Decrease
D.	Decrease	Increase

14. For a bond issue which sells for less than its par value,   14.___
    the market rate of interest is _____ rate stated on the
    bond.
    A. dependent on   B. equal to
    C. less than   D. higher than

15. Which of the following is GENERALLY associated with   15.___
    payables classified as accounts payable?

	Periodic payment of interest	Secured by collateral
A.	Yes	Yes
B.	Yes	No
C.	No	Yes
D.	No	No

16. An investor uses the cost method to account for invest-   16.___
    ments in common stock.
    Dividends received in excess of the investor's share of
    investee's earnings subsequent to the date of investment
    A. do not affect the investment account
    B. decrease the investment account
    C. increase the investment account
    D. increase the investment revenue account

17. A company has a marketable equity securities portfolio.   17.___
    The aggregate market value exceeds the aggregate cost.
    This difference should
       A. be accounted for as a valuation allowance in the
          asset section of the balance sheet
       B. be accounted for separately in the shareholders'
          equity section of the balance sheet
       C. be accounted for as an unrealized gain in the income
          statement
       D. not be accounted for in the financial statements

18. At the most recent year end, a company had a deferred   18.___
    income tax credit related to a current asset that exceeded
    a deferred income tax charge related to a current liabil-
    ity, and a deferred income tax credit related to a non-
    current asset.
    Which of the following should be reported in the company's
    MOST recent year-end balance sheet?
    The
       A. sum of the two deferred income tax credits as a
          noncurrent liability
       B. excess of the two deferred income tax credits over
          the deferred income tax charge as a current
          liability
       C. excess of the deferred income tax credit related to
          a current asset over the deferred income tax charge
          related to a current liability as a current
          liability
       D. deferred income tax charge as a current asset

19. A company with an effective income tax rate of 40% should   19.___
    report in its balance sheet a noncurrent deferred income
    tax credit for
       A. the total amount of the excess of accumulated depre-
          ciation for financial statement purposes over
          accumulated depreciation for income tax purposes
       B. 40% of the excess of accumulated depreciation for
          financial statement purposes over accumulated depre-
          ciation for income tax purposes
       C. the total amount of the excess of accumulated depre-
          ciation for income tax purposes over accumulated
          depreciation for financial statement purposes
       D. 40% of the excess of accumulated depreciation for
          income tax purposes over accumulated depreciation
          for financial statement purposes

20. Which of the following costs of internally generated   20.___
    goodwill inherent in a continuing business and related
    to an enterprise as a whole should be capitalized and
    then amortized over their estimated useful lives?

	Costs of maintaining goodwill	Costs of restoring goodwill
A.	Yes	Yes
B.	Yes	No
C.	No	Yes
D.	No	No

21. Theoretically, which of the following costs incurred in connection with a machine purchased for use in a company's manufacturing operations would be capitalized?

	Insurance on machine while in transit	Testing and preparation of machine for use
A.	No	No
B.	No	Yes
C.	Yes	No
D.	Yes	Yes

21.____

22. A machine with a four-year estimated useful life and an estimated 15% salvage value was acquired on January 1, 1991.
The increase in accumulated depreciation for 1992 using the double-declining-balance method would be
Original cost ×
A. 85% × 50%
B. 50%
C. 85% × 50% × 50%
D. 50% × 50%

22.____

23. An expenditure subsequent to acquisition of assembly-line manufacturing equipment benefits future periods. The expenditure should be capitalized if it is a

	Betterment	Rearrangement
A.	No	No
B.	No	Yes
C.	Yes	No
D.	Yes	Yes

23.____

24. The replacement cost of an inventory item is below the net realizable value and above the net realizable value less the normal profit margin. The original cost of the inventory item is above the replacement cost and below the net realizable value.
As a result, under the lower of cost or market method, the inventory item should be valued at the
   A. original cost
   B. replacement cost
   C. net realizable value
   D. net realizable value less the normal profit margin

24.____

25. The dollar-value LIFO inventory cost flow method involves computations based on

	Inventory pools of similar items	A specific price index for each year
A.	No	Yes
B.	No	No
C.	Yes	No
D.	Yes	Yes

25.____

26. Theoretically, warehousing costs incurred by the consignor before consigned goods are transferred to the consignee should be considered
   A. an expense by the consignor
   B. an expense by the consignee
   C. inventoriable by the consignor
   D. inventoriable by the consignee

26.____

27. When measuring the current cost of inventories in accordance with FASB Statement No. 33, the date of sale is the   27.___

	Entry date	Exit date
A.	No	Yes
B.	Yes	Yes
C.	Yes	No
D.	No	No

28. A subsidiary, acquired for cash in a business combination, owned inventories with a market value different than the book value as of the date of combination. A consolidated balance sheet prepared immediately after the acquisition would include this difference as part of   28.___
    A. deferred credits   B. goodwill
    C. inventories   D. retained earnings

29. According to the FASB Conceptual Framework, which of the following relates to both relevance and reliability?   29.___

	Consistency	Verifiability
A.	Yes	Yes
B.	Yes	No
C.	No	Yes
D.	No	No

30. According to the FASB Conceptual Framework, earnings   30.___
    A. are the same as comprehensive income
    B. exclude certain gains and losses that are included in comprehensive income
    C. include certain gains and losses that are excluded from comprehensive income
    D. include certain losses that are excluded from comprehensive income

KEY (CORRECT ANSWERS)

1. A	11. A	21. D
2. D	12. D	22. D
3. A	13. C	23. D
4. A	14. D	24. B
5. A	15. D	25. D
6. A	16. B	26. C
7. D	17. D	27. A
8. C	18. C	28. C
9. D	19. D	29. B
10. C	20. D	30. B

FINANCIAL MANAGEMENT

Contents

FINANCIAL MANAGEMENT

I. The Necessity of Financial Planning

There is one simple reason to understand and observe financial planning in your business—to avoid failure. Eight of ten new businesses fail primarily because of the lack of good financial planning.

Financial planning affects how and on what terms you will be able to attract the funding required to establish, maintain, and expand your business. Financial planning determines the raw materials you can afford to buy, the products you will be able to produce, and whether or not you will be able to market them efficiently. It affects the human and physical resources you will be able to acquire to operate your business. It will be a major determinant of whether or not you will be able to make your hard work profitable.

This manual provides an overview of the essential components of financial planning and management. Used wisely, it will make the reader—the small business owner/manager—familiar enough with the fundamentals to have a fighting chance of success in today's highly competitive business environment.

A clearly conceived, well documented financial plan, establishing goals and including the use of Pro Forma Statements and Budgets to ensure financial control, will demonstrate not only that you know what you want to do, but that you know how to accomplish it. This demonstration is essential to attract the capital required by your business from creditors and investors.

What Is Financial Management?

Very simply stated, financial management is the use of financial statements that reflect the financial condition of a business to identify its relative strengths and weaknesses. It enables you to plan, using projections, future financial performance for capital, asset, and personnel requirements to maximize the return on shareholders' investment.

Tools of Financial Planning

This manual introduces the tools required to prepare a financial plan for your business's development, including the following:

• Basic Financial Statements—the Balance Sheet and Statement of Income

• Ratio Analysis—a means by which individual business performance is compared to similar businesses in the same category

• The Pro Forma Statement of Income—a method used to forecast future profitability

• Break-Even Analysis—a method allowing the small business person to calculate the sales level at which a business recovers all

2

its costs or expenses

• The Cash Flow Statement—also known as the Budget identifies the flow of cash into and out of the business

• Pricing formulas and policies—used to calculate profitable selling prices for products and services

• Types and sources of capital available to finance business operations

• Short- and long-term planning considerations necessary to maximize profits

The business owner/manager who understands these concepts and uses them effectively to control the evolution of the business is practicing sound financial management thereby increasing the likelihood of success.

II. Understanding Financial Statements: A Health Checkup for Your Business

Financial Statements record the performance of your business and allow you to diagnose its strengths and weaknesses by providing a written summary of financial activities. There are two primary financial statements: the Balance Sheet and the Statement of Income.

The Balance Sheet

The Balance Sheet provides a picture of the financial health of a business at a given moment, usually at the **close** of an accounting period. It lists in detail **those** material and intangible items the business **owns** (known as its *assets*) and what money the business **owes**, either to its creditors (*liabilities*) or to its owners (*shareholders' equity* or *net worth* of the business).

Assets include not only cash, merchandise inventory, land, buildings, equipment, machinery, furniture, patents, trademarks, and the like, but also money due from individuals or other businesses (known as *accounts* or *notes receivable*).

Liabilities are funds acquired for a business through loans or the sale of property or services to the business on credit. Creditors do not acquire business ownership, but promissory notes to be paid at a designated future date.

Shareholders' equity (or *net worth* or *capital*) is money put into a business by its owners for use by the business in acquiring assets.

At any given time, a business's assets equal the total contributions by the creditors and owners, as illustrated by the following formula for the Balance Sheet:

Assets	=	**Liabilities**	+	**Net Worth**
(Total funds invested in assets of the business)		(Funds supplied to the business by its creditors)		(Funds supplied to the business by its owners)

This formula is a basic premise of accounting. If a business owes more money to creditors than it possesses in value of assets owned, the net worth or owner's equity of the business will be a negative number.

The Balance Sheet is designed to show how the assets, liabilities, and net worth of a business are distributed at any given time. It is usually prepared at regular intervals; e.g., at each month's end, but especially at the end of each fiscal (accounting) year.

By regularly preparing this summary of what the business owns and owes (the Balance Sheet), the business owner/manager can identify and analyze trends in the financial strength of the business. It permits timely modifications, such as gradually decreasing the amount of money the business owes to creditors and increasing the amount the business owes its owners.

All Balance Sheets contain the same categories of assets, liabilities, and net worth. Assets are arranged in decreasing order of how quickly they can be turned into cash (*liquidity*). Liabilities are listed in order of how soon they must be repaid, followed by retained earnings (net worth or owner's equity), as illustrated in Figure 2-1, the sample Balance Sheet for ABC Company.

The categories and format of the Balance Sheet are established by a system known as Generally Accepted Accounting Principles (GAAP). The system is applied to all companies, large or small, so anyone reading the Balance Sheet can readily understand the story it tells.

Balance Sheet Categories
Assets and liabilities are broken down into categories as described on page 8.

Figure 2-1

ABC Company

December 31, 19____

Balance Sheet

Cash	$1,896	Notes Payable, Bank	$2,000
Accounts Receivable	1,456	Accounts Payable	2,240
Inventory	6,822	Accruals	940
Total Current Assets	$10,174	Total Current Liabilities	$5,180
Equipment and Fixtures	1,168	Total Liabilities	5,180
Prepaid Expenses	1,278	Net Worth*	7,440
Total Assets	$12,620	Total Liabilities and New Worth	$12,620

*Assets – Liabilities = New Worth

Assets: An asset is anything the business owns that has monetary value.

- *Current Assets* include cash, government securities, marketable securities, accounts receivable, notes receivable (other than from officers or employees), inventories, prepaid expenses, and any other item that could be converted into cash within one year in the normal course of business.

- *Fixed Assets* are those acquired for long-term use in a business such as land, plant, equipment, machinery, leasehold improvements, furniture, fixtures, and any other items with an expected useful business life measured in *years* (as opposed to items that will wear out or be used up in less than one y ar and are usually expensed when they are purchased). These assets are typically not for resale and are recorded in the Balance Sheet at their net cost less accumulated depreciation.

- *Other Assets* include intangible assets, such as patents, royalty arrangements, copyrights, exclusive use contracts, and notes receivable from officers and employees.

Liabilities: Liabilities are the claims of creditors against the assets of the business (debts owed by the business).

- *Current Liabilities* are accounts payable, notes payable to banks, accrued expenses (wages, salaries), taxes payable, the current portion (due within one year) of long-term debt, and other obligations to creditors due within one year.

- *Long-Term Liabilities* are mortgages, intermediate and long-term bank loans, equipment loans, and any other obligation for money due to a creditor with a maturity longer than one year.

- *Net Worth* is the assets of the business minus its liabilities. Net worth equals the owner's equity. This equity is the investment by the owner plus any profits or minus any losses that have accumulated in the business.

The Statement of Income

The second primary report included in a business's Financial Statement is the Statement of Income. The Statement of Income is a measurement of a company's sales and expenses over a specific period of time. It is also prepared at regular intervals (again, each month and fiscal year end) to show the results of operating during those accounting periods. It too follows Generally Accepted Accounting Principles (GAAP) and contains specific revenue and expense categories regardless of the nature of the business.

Statement of Income Categories
The Statement of Income categories are calculated as described below:

- *Net Sales* (gross sales less returns and allowances)

- Less *Cost of Goods Sold* (cost of inventories)

- Equals *Gross Margin* (gross profit on sales before operating expenses)

- Less *Selling and Administrative Expenses* (salaries, wages, payroll taxes and benefits, rent, utilities, maintenance expenses, office supplies, postage, automobile/vehicle expenses, insurance, legal and accounting expenses, depreciation)

- Equals *Operating Profit* (profit before other non-operating income or expense)

- Plus *Other Income* (income from discounts, investments, customer charge accounts)

- Less *Other Expenses* (interest expense)

- Equals *Net Profit* (Loss) Before Tax (the figure on which your tax is calculated)

- Less *Income Taxes* (if any are due)

- Equals *Net Profit (Loss) After Tax*

For an example of a Statement of Income, see Figure 2-2 the statement of ABC Company.

Figure 2-2
ABC Company
December 31, 19____
Income Statement

Net Sales		$68,116
Cost of Goods Sold		47,696
Gross Profit on Sales		$20,420
Expenses		
Wages	$6,948	
Delivery Expenses	954	
Bad Debts Allowances	409	
Communications	204	
Depreciation Allowance	409	
Insurance	613	
Taxes	1,021	
Advertising	1,566	
Interest	409	
Other Charges	749	
Total Expenses		$13,282
Net Profit		7,138
Other Income		886
Total Net Income		$8,024

Calculating the Cost of Goods Sold

Calculation of the Cost of Goods Sold category in the Statement of Income (or Profit-and-Loss Statement as it is sometimes called) varies depending on whether the business is retail, wholesale, or manufacturing. In retailing and wholesaling, computing the cost of goods sold during the accounting period involves beginning and ending inventories. This, of course, includes purchases made during the accounting period. In manufacturing it involves not only finished-goods inventories, but also raw materials inventories, goods-in-process inventories, direct labor, and direct factory overhead costs. *

Regardless of the calculation for Cost of Goods Sold, deduct the Cost of Goods Sold from Net Sales to get Gross Margin or Gross Profit. From Gross Profit, deduct general or indirect overhead, such as selling expenses, office expenses, and interest expenses, to calculate your Net Profit. This is the final profit after all costs and expenses for the accounting period have been deducted.

*The Handbook of Small Business Finance, U.S. Small Business Administration Small Business Management Series No. 15 has excellent illustrations of the different methods of calculation for the Cost of Goods Sold for the various business types.

III. Financial Ratio Analysis

The Balance Sheet and the Statement of Income are essential, but they are only the starting point for successful financial management. Apply Ratio Analysis to Financial Statements to analyze the success, failure, and progress of your business.

Ratio Analysis enables the business owner/manager to spot trends in a business and to compare its performance and condition with the average performance of similar businesses in the same industry. To do this compare your ratios with the average of businesses similar to yours and compare your own ratios for several successive years, watching especially for any unfavorable trends that may be starting. Ratio analysis may provide the all-important early warning indications that allow you to solve your business problems before your business is destroyed by them.

Balance Sheet Ratio Analysis

Important Balance Sheet Ratios measure liquidity and solvency (a business's ability to pay its bills as they come due) and leverage (the extent to which the business is dependent on creditors' funding). They include the following ratios:

Liquidity Ratios.
These ratios indicate the ease of turning assets into cash. They include the Current Ratio, Quick Ratio, and Working Capital.

Current Ratios. The Current Ratio is one of the best known measures of financial strength. It is figured as shown below:

$$\text{Current Ratio} = \frac{\text{Total Current Assets}}{\text{Total Current Liabilities}}$$

The main question this ratio addresses is: "Does your business have enough current assets to meet the payment schedule of its current debts with a margin of safety for possible losses in current assets, such as inventory shrinkage or collectable accounts?" A generally acceptable current ratio is 2 to 1. But whether or not a specific ratio is satisfactory depends on the nature of the business and the characteristics of its current assets and liabilities. The minimum acceptable current ratio is obviously 1:1, but that relationship is usually playing it too close for comfort.

If you decide your business's current ratio is too low, you may be able to raise it by:

• Paying some debts.

• Increasing your current assets from loans or other borrowings with a maturity of more than one year.

• Converting noncurrent assets into current assets.

14

• Increasing your current assets from new equity contributions.

• Putting profits back into the business.

Quick Ratios. The Quick Ratio is sometimes called the "acid-test" ratio and is one of the best measures of liquidity. It is figured as shown below:

$$\text{Quick Ratio} = \frac{\text{Cash} + \text{Government Securities} + \text{Receivables}}{\text{Total Current Liabilities}}$$

The Quick Ratio is a much more exacting measure than the Current Ratio. By excluding inventories, it concentrates on the really liquid assets, with value that is fairly certain. It helps answer the question: "If all sales revenues should disappear, could my business meet its current obligations with the readily convertible 'quick' funds on hand?"

An acid-test of 1:1 is considered satisfactory unless the majority of your "quick assets" are in accounts receivable, and the pattern of accounts receivable collection lags behind the schedule for paying current liabilities.

Working Capital. Working Capital is more a measure of *cash flow* than a ratio. The result of this calculation **must** be a positive number. It is calculated as shown below:

$$\text{Working Capital} = \text{Total Current Assets} - \text{Total Current Liabilities}$$

Bankers look at Net Working Capital over time to determine a company's ability to weather financial crises. Loans are often tied to minimum working capital requirements.

A general observation about these three Liquidity Ratios is that the higher they are the better, especially if you are relying to any significant extent on creditor money to finance assets.

Leverage Ratio
This Debt/Worth or Leverage Ratio indicates the extent to which the business is reliant on debt financing (creditor money versus owner's equity):

$$\textbf{Debt/Worth Ratio} = \frac{\text{Total Liabilities}}{\text{Net Worth}}$$

Generally, the higher this ratio, the more risky a creditor will perceive its exposure in your business, making it correspondingly harder to obtain credit.

Income Statement Ratio Analysis

The following important State of Income Ratios measure profitability:

Gross Margin Ratio
This ratio is the percentage of sales dollars left after subtracting the cost of goods sold from net sales. It measures the percentage of sales dollars remaining (after obtaining or manufacturing the goods sold) available to pay the overhead expenses of the

16

company.

Comparison of your business ratios to those of similar businesses will reveal the relative strengths or weaknesses in your business. The Gross Margin Ratio is calculated as follows:

$$\textbf{Gross Margin Ratio} = \frac{\text{Gross Profit}}{\text{Net Sales}}$$

(Gross Profit = Net Sales − Cost of Goods Sold)

Net Profit Margin Ratio

This ratio is the percentage of sales dollars left after subtracting the Cost of Goods sold and all expenses, except income taxes. It provides a good opportunity to compare your company's "return on sales" with the performance of other companies in your industry. It is calculated **before** income tax because tax rates and tax liabilities vary from company to company for a wide variety of reasons, making comparisons after taxes much more difficult. The Net Profit Margin Ratio is calculated as follows:

$$\textbf{Net Profit Margin Ratio} = \frac{\text{Net Profit Before Tax}}{\text{Net Sales}}$$

Management Ratios

Other important ratios, often referred to as Management Ratios, are also derived from Balance Sheet and Statement of Income information.

Inventory Turnover Ratio

This ratio reveals how well inventory is being managed. It is important because the more times inventory can be turned in a given operating cycle, the greater the profit. The Inventory Turnover Ratio is calculated as follows:

$$\text{Inventory Turnover Ratio} = \frac{\text{Net Sales}}{\text{Average Inventory at Cost}}$$

Accounts Receivable Turnover Ratio

This ratio indicates how well accounts receivable are being collected. If receivables are not collected reasonably in accordance with their terms, management should rethink its collection policy. If receivables are excessively slow in being converted to cash, liquidity could be severely impaired. The Accounts Receivable Turnover Ratio is calculated as follows:

$$\frac{\text{Net Credit Sales/Year}}{365 \text{ Days/Year}} = \text{Daily Credit Sales}$$

$$\text{Accounts Receivable Turnover (in days)} = \frac{\text{Accounts Receivable}}{\text{Daily Credit Sales}}$$

Return on Assets Ratio

This measures how efficiently profits are being generated from the assets employed in the business when compared with the ratios of firms in a similar business. A low ratio in comparison with industry averages indicates an inefficient use of business assets. The Return on Assets Ratio is calculated as follows:

$$\text{Return on Assets} = \frac{\text{Net Profit Before Tax}}{\text{Total Assets}}$$

Return on Investment (ROI) Ratio.
The ROI is perhaps the most important ratio of all. It is the percentage of return on funds invested in the business by its owners. In short, this ratio tells the owner whether or not all the effort put into the business has been worthwhile. If the ROI is less than the rate of return on an alternative, risk-free investment such as a bank savings account or certificate of deposit, the owner may be wiser to sell the company, put the money in such a savings instrument, and avoid the daily struggles of small business management. The ROI is calculated as follows:

$$\text{Return on Investment} = \frac{\text{Net Profit before Tax}}{\text{Net Worth}}$$

These Liquidity, Leverage, Profitability, and Management Ratios* allow the business owner to identify trends in a business and to compare its progress with the performance of others through data published by various sources. The owner may thus determine the business's relative strengths and weaknesses.

Sources of Comparative Information

Sources of comparative financial information which you may obtain from your public library or the publishers include the following:

Almanac of Business and Industrial Financial Ratios, Leo Troy, Prentice-Hall, Inc., Englewood Cliffs, NJ 07632

---

*An excellent discussion of other ratio analysis methods may be found in Chapter 3 of the U.S. Small Business Administration Management Series (SBMS) No. 15 *Handbook of Small Business Finance* and on the concept of Return on Investment in Chapter 7 of the U.S. Small Business Management Series No. 25, *Guide for Profit Planning*. Further discussion of ratio analysis and detailed lists of business ratio sources can be found in SBMS No. 20, *Ratio Analysis for Small Business*.

Annual Statement Studies, Robert Morris Associates, P. O. Box 8500, S-1140, Philadelphia, PA 19178

Expenses in Retail Business, National Cash Register Corporation, Corporate Advertising and Sales Promotion, Dayton, OH 45479.

Key Business Ratios, Dun & Bradstreet, Inc., 99 Church Street, New York, NY 10007, ATTN: Public Relations and Advertising Department

IV. Forecasting Profits

Forecasting, particularly on a short-term basis (one year to three years), is essential to planning for business success. This process, estimating future business performance based on the actual results from prior periods, enables the business owner/manager to modify the operation of the business on a timely basis. This allows the business to avoid losses or major financial problems should some future results from operations not conform with reasonable expectations. Forecasts—or Pro Forma Income Statements and Cash Flow Statements as they are usually called—also provide the most persuasive management tools to apply for loans or attract investor money. As a business expands, there will inevitably be a need for more money than can be internally generated from profits.

Facts Affecting Pro Forma Statements

Preparation of Forecasts (Pro Forma Statements) requires assembling a wide array of pertinent, verifiable facts affecting your business and its past performance. These include:

- Data from prior financial statements, particularly:
  a. Previous sales levels and trends
  b. Past gross percentages
  c. Average past general, administrative, and selling expenses necessary to generate your former sales volumes
  d. Trends in the company's need to borrow (supplier, trade credit, and bank credit) to support various levels of inventory and trends in accounts receivable required to achieve previous sales volumes

- Unique company data, particularly:
  a. Plant capacity
  b. Competition
  c. Financial constraints
  d. Personnel availability

- Industry-wide factors, including:
  a. Overall state of the economy
  b. Economic status of your industry within the economy
  c. Population growth
  d. Elasticity* of demand for the product or service your business provides
  e. Availability of raw materials

Once these factors are identified, they may be used in Pro Formas, which estimate the level of sales, expense, and profitability that seem possible in a future period of operations.

The Pro Forma Income Statement

In preparing the Pro Forma Income Statement, the estimate of total sales during a selected period is the most critical

---

*Demand is said to be "elastic" if it decreases as prices increase, a demonstration that consumers can do without or with less of the goods or service. If demand for something is relatively steady as prices increase, it is "inelastic."

"guesstimate." Employ business experience from past financial statements. Get help from management and salespeople in developing this all-important number.

Then assume, for example, that a 10 percent increase in sales volume is a realistic and attainable goal. Multiply last year's net sales by 1.10 to get this year's estimate of total net sales. Next, break down this total, month by month, by looking at the historical monthly sales volume. From this you can determine what percentage of total annual sales fell on the average in each of those months over a minimum of the past three years. You may find that 75 percent of total annual sales volume was realized during the six months from July through December in each of those years and that the remaining 25 percent of sales was spread fairly evenly over the first six months of the year.

Next, estimate the cost of goods sold by analyzing operating data to determine on a monthly basis what percentage of sales has gone into cost of goods sold in the past. This percentage can then be adjusted for expected variations in costs, price trends, and efficiency of operations.

Operating expenses (sales, general and administrative expenses, depreciation, and interest), other expenses, other income, and taxes can then be estimated through detailed analysis and adjustment of what they were in the past and what you expect them to be in the future.

Comparison with Actual Monthly Performance

Putting together this information month by month for a year into the future will result in your business's Pro Forma Statement of Income. Use it to compare with the actual monthly results from operations by using the SBA form 1099 (4-82) *Operating Plan Forecast (Profit and Loss Projection)*. Obtain this form from your

local SBA office. You will find it helpful to refer to the SBA
Guidelines for Profit and Loss Projection. Preparation of the
information is summarized below and on the back of the form
1099.

Revenue (Sales)

• List the departments within the business. For example, if your
business is appliance sales and service, the departments would
include new appliances, used appliances, parts, in-shop service,
on-site service.

• In the "Estimate" columns, enter a reasonable projection of
monthly sales for each department of the business. Include cash
and on-account sales. In the "Actual" columns, enter the actual
sales for the month as they become available.

• Exclude from the Revenue section any revenue not strictly
related to the business.

Cost of Sales

• Cite costs by department of the business, as above.

• In the "Estimate" columns, enter the cost of sales estimated for
each month for each department. For product inventory, calculate
the cost of the goods sold for each department (beginning
inventory plus purchases and transportation costs during the
month minus the inventory). Enter "Actual" costs each month as
they accrue.

Gross Profit

• Subtract the total cost of sales from the total revenue.

Expenses

• Salary Expenses: Base pay plus overtime.

• Payroll Expenses: Include paid vacations, sick leave, health
insurance, unemployment insurance, Social Security taxes.

• Outside Services: Include costs of subcontracts, overflow work farmed-out, special or one-time services.

• Supplies: Services and items purchased for use in the business, not for resale.

• Repairs and Maintenance: Regular maintenance and repair, including periodic large expenditures, such as painting or decorating.

• Advertising: Include desired sales volume, classified directory listing expense, etc.

• Car, Delivery and Travel: Include charges if personal car is used in the business. Include parking, tolls, mileage on buying trips, repairs, etc.

• Accounting and Legal: Outside professional services.

• Rent: List only real estate used in the business.

• Telephone.

• Utilities: Water, heat, light, etc.

• Insurance: Fire or liability on property or products, worker's compensation.

• Taxes: Inventory, sales, excise, real estate, others.

• Interest.

• Depreciation: Amortization of capital assets.

• Other Expenses (specify each): Tools, leased equipment, etc.

• Miscellaneous (unspecied): Small expenditures without separate accounts.

Net Profit
• To find net profit, subtract total expenses from gross profit.

The Pro Forma Statement of Income, prepared on a monthly basis and culminating in an annual projection for the next business fiscal year, should be revised not less than quarterly. It must reflect the actual performance achieved in the immediately preceding three months to ensure its continuing usefulness as one of the two most valuable planning tools available to management. *

Should the Pro Forma reveal that the business will likely not generate a profit from operations, plans must immediately be developed to identify what to do to at least break even—increase volume, decrease expenses, or put more owner capital in to pay some debts and reduce interest expenses.

Break-Even Analysis

"Break-Even" means a level of operations at which a business neither makes a profit nor sustains a loss. At this point, revenue is just enough to cover expenses. Break-Even Analysis enables you to study the relationship of volume, costs, and revenue.

Break-Even requires the business owner/manager to define a sales level—either in terms of revenue dollars to be earned or in units to be sold within a given accounting period—at which the business would earn a before tax net profit of zero. This may be done by employing one of various formula calculations to the business estimated sales volume, estimated fixed costs, and estimated variable costs.

---

*A discussion of this complicated task is presented in the U.S. Small Business Management Series No. 15, *Guide for Profit Planning.*

Generally, the volume and cost estimates assume the following conditions:

• A change in sales volume will not affect the selling price per unit;

• Fixed expenses (rent, salaries, administrative and office expenses, interest, and depreciation) will remain the same at all volume levels; and

• Variable expenses (cost of goods sold, variable labor costs, including overtime wages and sales commissions) will increase or decrease in direct proportion to any increase or decrease in sales volume.

Two methods are generally employed in Break-Even Analysis, depending on whether the break-even point is calculated in terms of *sales dollar volume* or in *number of units* that must be sold.

Break-Even Point in Sales Dollars
The steps for calculating the first method are shown below:

1. Obtain a list of expenses incurred by the company during its past fiscal year.

2. Separate the expenses listed in Step 1 into either a *variable* or a *fixed* expense classification. (See Figure 4–1 under "Classification of Expenses.")

3. Express the variable expenses as a percentage of sales. In the condensed income statement (Figure 4–1) of the Small Business Specialities Co., net sales were $1,200,000. In Step 2, variable expenses were found to amount to $720,000. Therefore, variable expenses are 60 percent of net sales ($720,000 divided by $1,200,000). This means that 60 cents of every sales dollar is

required to cover variable expenses. Only the remainder, 40 cents of every dollar, is available for fixed expenses and profit.

4. Substitute the information gathered in the preceding steps in the following basic break-even formula to calculate the break-even point.

Figure 4-1

THE SMALL-BUSINESS SPECIALTIES CO.
Condensed Income Statement
For year ending Dec. 31, 19—

Net sales (60,000 units @ $20 per unit)		$1,200,000
Less cost of goods sold:		
Direct material	$195,000	
Direct labor	215,000	
Manufacturing expenses (Schedule A)	300,000	
Total		710,000
Gross profit		490,000
Less operating expenses:		
Selling expenses (Schedule B)	$200,000	
General and administrative expenses (Schedule C)	210,000	
Total		410,000
Net Income		$ 80,000

Supporting Schedules of Expenses Other Than Direct Material and Labor

	Total	Schedule A manufacturing expenses	Schedule B selling expenses	Schedule C general and administrative expenses
Rent	$ 60,000	$ 30,000	$ 8,000	$ 22,000
Insurance	11,000	9,000	1,000	1,000
Commissions	120,000	....	120,000	....
Property tax	12,000	10,000	1,000	1,000
Telephone	7,000	1,000	5,000	1,000
Depreciation	80,000	70,000	5,000	5,000
Power	100,000	100,000	....	....
Light	60,000	30,000	10,000	20,000
Officers' salaries	260,000	50,000	50,000	160,000
Total	$ 710,000	$ 300,000	$ 200,000	$ 210,000

Classification of Expenses

	Total	Variable	Fixed
Direct material	$ 195,000	195,000	....
Direct labor	215,000	215,000	....
Manufacturing expenses	300,000	100,000	$200,000
Selling expenses	200,000		50,000
General and administrative expenses	210,000	60,000	150,000
Total	$1,120,000	$720,000	$400,000

where: S = F + V (Sales at the break-even point)
    F = Fixed expenses
    V = Variable expenses expressed as a percentage of
        sales.

This formula means that when sales revenues equal the fixed
expenses and variable expenses incurred in producing the sales
revenues, there will be no profit or loss. At this point, revenue
from sales is just sufficient to cover the fixed and the variable
expenses. In this formula "S" is the *break-even point*.

For the Small Business Specialties Co., the break-even point (using
the basic formula and data from Figure 3–2) may be calculated as
follows:

$$S = F + V$$
$$S = \$400,000 + 0.60S$$
$$10S = \$4,000,000 + 6S^*$$
$$10S - 6S = \$4,000,000$$
$$4S = \$4,000,000$$
$$S = \$1,000,000$$

Proof that this calculation is correct follows:

Sales at break-even point per calculation $1,000,000
Less variable expenses (60 percent of sales) . . .   600,000
Marginal income   400,000
Less fixed expenses.   400,000
Equals neither profit nor loss $ 0

---

*Both sides of the equation were multiplied by 10 to eliminate decimal fractions.

Modification: Break-Even Point to Obtain Desired Net Income.
The first break-even formula can be modified to show the dollar
sales required to obtain a certain amount of desired net income.
To do this, let "S" mean the *sales required to obtain a certain
amount of net income*, say $80,000. The formula then reads:

$$S = F + V + \text{Desired Net Income}$$
$$S = \$400,000 + 0.60S + \$80,000$$
$$10S = \$4,000,000 + 6S + 800,000*$$
$$4S = \$4,800,000$$
$$S = \$1,200,000$$

Break-Even Point in Units to be Sold
You may want to calculate the break-even point in terms of units
to be sold instead of sales dollars. If so, a second formula (in
which "S" means *units to be sold* to break even) may be used:

$$\text{Break-even Sales} = \frac{\text{Fixed expenses}}{\text{Unit sales price} - \text{Unit variable expenses}}$$
$$(S = \text{Units})$$

$$S = \frac{\$400,000}{\$20 - \$12} = \frac{\$400,000}{\$8}$$

$$S = 50,000 \text{ units}$$

The Small Business Specialties Co. must sell 50,000 units at $20
per unit to break even under the assumptions contained in this
illustration. The sale of 50,000 units at $20 each equals $1 million,
the break-even sales volume in dollars calculated in the basic
formula. This formula indicates there is $8 per unit of sales that
can be used to cover the $400,000 fixed expense. Then $400 000
divided by $8 gives the number of units required to break even.

31

Modification: Break-Even Point in Units to be Sold to Obtain Desired Net Income. The second formula can be modified to show the number of units required to obtain a certain amount of net income. In this case, let S mean the number of units required to obtain a certain amount of net income, again say $80,000. The formula then reads as follows:

$$S = \frac{\text{Fixed expenses} + \text{Net income}}{\text{Unit sales price} - \text{Unit variable expense}}$$

$$S = \frac{\$400,000 + \$80,000}{\$20 - \$12} = \frac{\$480,000}{\$8}$$

$$S = 60,000 \text{ units}$$

Break-even Analysis may also be represented graphically by charting the sales dollars or sales units required to break even as in Figure 4-2.

Remember: Increased sales do not necessarily mean increased profits. If you know your company's break-even point, you will know how to price your product to make a profit. If you cannot make an acceptable profit, alter or sell your business before you lose your retained earnings. *

---

*An extensive discussion of Break-Even Analysis is also contained in the *Guides for Profit Planning*, U.S. Small Business Management Series No. 25, from which these break-even method explanations were excerpted.

Figure 4-2

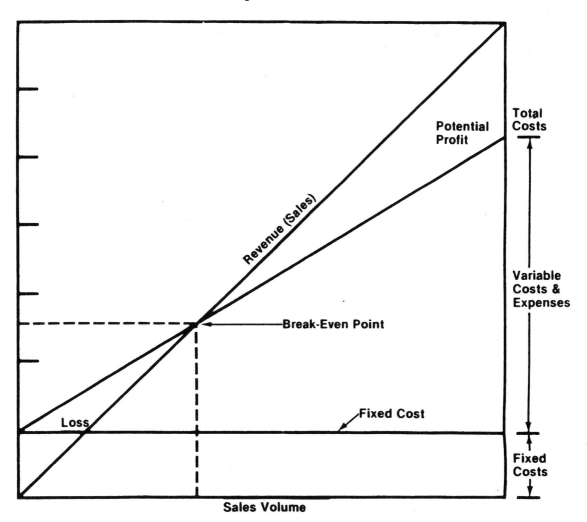

Sales Volume

V. Cash Flow Management: Budgeting and Controlling Costs

If there is anything more important to the successful financial management of a business than the thorough, thoughtful preparation of Pro Forma Income Statements, it is the preparation of the Cash Flow Statement, sometimes called the Cash Flow Budget.

The Cash Flow Statement

The Cash Flow Statement identifies when cash is expected to be received and when it must be spent to pay bills and debts. It shows how much cash will be needed to pay expenses and when it will be needed. It also allows the manager to identify where the necessary cash will come from. For example, will it be internally generated from sales and the collection of accounts receivable—or must it be borrowed? (The Cash Flow Projection deals only with actual cash transactions; depreciation and amortization of good

34

will or other non-cash expense items are not considered in this Pro Forma.)

The Cash Flow Statement, based on management estimates of sales and obligations, identifies when money will be flowing into and out of the business. It enables management to plan for shortfalls in cash resources so short term working capital loans may be arranged in advance. It allows management to schedule purchases and payments in a way that enables the business to borrow as little as possible. Because all sales are not cash sales, management must be able to forecast when accounts receivable will become "cash in the bank" and when expenses—whether regular or seasonal—must be paid so cash shortfalls will not interrupt normal business operations.

The Cash Flow Statement may also be used as a Budget, permitting the manager increased control of the business through continuous comparison of actual receipts and disbursements against forecast amounts. This comparison helps the small business owner identify areas for timely improvement in financial management.

By closely watching the timing of cash receipts and disbursements, cash balance on hand, and loan balances, management can readily identify such things as deficiencies in collecting receivables, unrealistic trade credit or loan repayment schedules. Surplus cash that may be invested on a short-term basis or used to reduce debt and interest expenses temporarily can be recognized. In short, it is the most valuable tool management has at its disposal to refine the day-to-day operation of a business. It is an important financial tool bank lenders evaluate when a business needs a loan, for it demonstrates not only how large a loan is required but also when and how it can be repaid.

A Cash Flow Statement or Budget can be prepared for any period of time. However, a one-year budget matching the fiscal year of your business is recommended. As in the preparation and use of the Pro Forma Statement of Income, the projected Cash Flow Statement should be prepared on a monthly basis for the next year. It should be revised not less than quarterly to reflect actual performance in the preceding three months of operations to check its projections.

In preparing the Cash Flow Statement or Budget start with the sales budget. Other budgets are related directly or indirectly to this budget. The following is a sales forecast in units:

Sales Budget—Units
For the Year Ended December 31, 19 ____

Territory	Total	1st Quarter	2nd Quarter	3rd Quarter	4th Quarter
East.	26,000	5,000	6,000	7,000	8,000
West.	11,000	2,000	2,500	3,000	3,500
	37,000	7,000	8,500	10,000	11,500

Assume you sell a single product and the sales price for it is $10. Your sales budget in terms of dollars would look like this:

Sales Budget—Dollars
For the Year Ended December 31, 19 ____

Territory	Total	1st Quarter	2nd Quarter	3rd Quarter	4th Quarter
East.	$260,000	$50,000	$80,000	$ 70,000	$ 80,000
West.	110,000	20,000	25,000	30,000	35,000
	$370,000	$70,000	$85,000	$100,000	$115,000

Say the estimated per unit cost of the product is $1.50 for direct material, $2.50 for direct labor, and $1.00 for manufacturing overhead. By applying unit costs to the sales budget in units, you would come out with this budget:

Cost of Goods Sold Budget
For the Year Ended December 31, 19 ____

	Total	1st Quarter	2nd Quarter	3rd Quarter	4th Quarter
Direct material	$ 55,500	$10,500	$12,750	$15,000	$17,250
Direct labor	92,500	17,500	21,250	25,000	28,750
Mfg. overhead	37,000	7,000	8,500	10,000	11,500
	$185,000	$35,000	$42,500	$50,000	$57,500

Later on, before a cash budget can be compiled, you will need to know the estimated cash requirements for selling expenses. Therefore, you prepare a budget for selling expenses and another for cash expenditures for selling expenses (total selling expenses less depreciation):

Selling Expenses Budget
For the Year Ended December 31, 19 ____

	Total	1st Quarter	2nd Quarter	3rd Quarter	4th Quarter
Commissions................	$46,500	$ 8,750	$10,625	$12,500	$14,375
Rent	9,250	1,750	2,125	2,500	2,875
Advertising.................	9,250	1,750	2,125	2,500	2,875
Telephone..................	4,625	875	1,062	1,250	1,437
Depreciation—office	900	225	225	225	225
Other	22,250	4,150	5,088	6,025	6,983
	$92,500	$17,500	$21,250	$25,000	$28,750

Selling Expenses Budget—Cash Requirements
For the Year Ended December 31, 19 ____

	Total	1st Quarter	2nd Quarter	3rd Quarter	4th Quarter
Total selling expenses	$92,500	$17,500	$21,250	$25,000	$28,750
Less: depreciation .... expense-office	900	225	225	225	225
Cash requirements	$91,600	$17,275	$21,025	$24,775	$28,525

Basic information for an estimate of administrative expenses for the coming year is easily compiled. Again, from that budget you can estimate cash requirements for those expenses to be used subsequently in preparing the cash budget.

Administrative Expenses Budget
For the Year Ended December 31, 19 ____

	Total	1st Quarter	2nd Quarter	3rd Quarter	4th Quarter
Salaries....................	$22,200	$4,200	$5,100	$ 6,000	$ 6,900
Insurance	1,850	350	425	500	575
Telephone.................	1,850	350	425	500	575
Supplies....................	3,700	700	850	1,000	1,150
Bad debt expenses..........	3,700	700	850	1,000	1,150
Other expenses	3,700	700	850	1,000	1,150
	$37,000	$7,000	$8,500	$10,000	$11,500

Administrative Expenses Budget—Cash Requirements
For the Year Ended December 31, 19 ____

	Total	1st Quarter	2nd Quarter	3rd Quarter	4th Quarter
Estimated adm. expenses	$37,000	$7,000	$8,500	$10,000	$11,500
Less: bad debt expenses......	3,700	700	850	1,000	1,150
Cash requirements	$33.300	$6,500	$7,650	$ 9,000	$10,350

Now, from the information budgeted so far, you can proceed to prepare the budget income statement. Assume you plan to borrow $10,000 at the end of the first quarter. Although payable at maturity of the note, the interest appears in the last three quarters of the year. The statement will resemble the following:

Budgeted Income Statement
For the Year Ended December 31, 19 ____

	Total	1st Quarter	2nd Quarter	3rd Quarter	4th Quarter
Sales......................	$370,000	$70,000	$85,000	$100,000	$115,000
Cost of goods sold............	185,000	35,000	42,500	50,000	57,500
Gross Margin...............	$185,000	$35,000	$42,500	$ 50,000	$ 57,500
Operating expenses:					
Selling	$ 92,500	$17,500	$21,250	$ 25,000	$ 28,750
Administrative............	37,000	7,000	8,500	$ 10,000	$ 11,500
Total..................	$129,500	$24,500	$29,750	$ 35,000	$ 40,250
Net income					
from operations............	$ 55,500	$10,500	$12,750	$ 15,000	$ 17,250
Interest expense	450		150	150	150
Net income before					
income taxes	$ 55,050	$10,500	$12,600	$ 14,850	$ 17,100
Federal income tax........	27,525	5,250	6,300	7,425	8,550
Net income	$ 27,525	$ 5,250	$ 6,300	$ 7,425	$ 8,550

Estimating that 90 percent of your account sales is collected in the quarter in which they are made, that 9 percent is collected in the quarter following the quarter in which the sales were made, and that 1 percent of account sales is uncollectible, your accounts receivable budget of collections would look like this:

Budget of Collections of Accounts Receivable
For the Year Ended December 31, 19 ____

	Total (net)	1st Quarter	2nd Quarter	3rd Quarter	4th Quarter
4th Quarter Sales 19-0.......	$ 6,000	$ 6,000			
1st Quarter Sales 19-1	69,300	63,000	$ 6,300		
2nd Quarter Sales 19-1	84,150		76,500	$ 7,650	
3rd Quarter Sales 19-1.......	99,000			90,000	$ 9,000
4th Quarter Sales 19-1.......	103,500				103,500
	$361,950	$69,000	$82,800	$97,650	$112,500

Going back to the sales budget in units, now prepare a production budget in units. Assume you have 2,000 units in the opening

inventory and want to have on hand at the end of each quarter
the following quantities: 1st quarter, 3,000 units; 2nd quarter,
3,500 units; 3rd quarter, 4,000 units; and 4th quarter, 4,500 units.

Production Budget—Units
For the Year Ended December 31, 19 ____

	1st Quarter	2nd Quarter	3rd Quarter	4th Quarter
Sales requirements..............	7,000	8,500	10,000	11,500
Add: ending				
inventory requirements.........	3,000	3,500	4,000	4,500
Total requirements.............	10,000	12,500	14,000	16,000
Less: beginning				
inventory......................	2,000	3,000	3,500	4,000
Production				
requirements	8,000	9,000	10,500	112,000

Next, based on the production budget, prepare a budget to show
the purchases needed during each of the four quarters. Expressed
in terms of dollars, you do this by taking the production and
inventory figures and multiplying them by the cost of material
(previously estimated at $1.50 per unit). You could prepare a
similar budget expressed in units.

Budget of Direct Materials Purchases
For the Year Ended December 31, 19 ____

	1st Quarter	2nd Quarter	3rd Quarter	4th Quarter
Required for production	$12,000	$13,500	$15,750	$18,000
Required for ending inventory.....	4,500	5,250	6,000	6,750
Total.......................	$16,500	$18,750	$21,750	$24,750
Less: beginning inventory.........	3,000	4,500	5,250	6,000
Required purchases	$13,500	$14,250	$16,500	$18,750

Now suppose you pay 50 percent of your accounts in the quarter of the purchase and 50 percent in the following quarter. Carryover payables from last year were $5,000. Further, you always take the purchase discounts as a matter of good business policy. Since net purchases (less discount) were figured into the $1.50 cost estimate, purchase discounts do not appear in the budgets. Thus your payment on purchases budget will come out like this:

Payment on Purchases Budget
For the Year Ended December 31, 19 ____

	Total	1st Quarter	2nd Quarter	3rd Quarter	4th Quarter
4th Quarter Sales 19-0.......	$ 5,000	$ 5,000			
1st Quarter Sales 19-1.......	13,500	6,750	$ 6,750		
2nd Quarter Sales 19-1	14,250		7,125	$ 7.125	
3rd Quarter Sales 19-1.......	16,500			8,250	$ 8,250
4th Quarter Sales 19-1.......	9,375				9,375
Payments by Quarters......	$58,625	$11,750	$13,875	$15,375	$17,625

Taking the data for quantities produced from the production budget in units, calculate the direct labor requirements on the basis of units to be produced. (The number and cost of labor hours necessary to produce a given quantity can be set forth in supplemental schedules.)

Direct Labor Budget—Cash Requirements
For the Year Ended December 31, 19 ____

	Total	1st Quarter	2nd Quarter	3rd Quarter	4th Quarter
Quantity.....................	39,500	8,000	9,000	10,500	12,000
Direct labor cost.............	$98,750	$20,000	$22,500	$26,250	$30,000

Now outline the items that comprise your factory overhead, and prepare a budget like the following:

Manufacturing Overhead Budget
For the Year Ended December 31, 19 ____

	Total	1st Quarter	2nd Quarter	3rd Quarter	4th Quarter
Heat and power.............	$10,000	$1,000	$2,500	$ 3,000	$ 3,500
Factory supplies	5,300	1,000	1,500	1,800	1,000
Property taxes..............	2,000	500	500	500	500
Depreciation................	2,800	700	700	700	700
Rent	8,000	2,000	2,000	2,000	2,000
Superintendent	9,400	2,800	1,800	2,500	4,300
	$39,500	$8,000	$9,000	$10,500	$12,000

Figure the cash payments for manufacturing overhead by subtracting depreciation, which requires no cash outlay, from the totals above, and you will have the following breakdown:

Manufacturing Overhead Budget—Cash Requirements
For the Year Ended December 31, 19 ____

	Total	1st Quarter	2nd Quarter	3rd Quarter	4th Quarter
Productions—units	39,500	8,000	9,000	10,500	12,000
Mfg. overhead expenses	$39,500	$8,000	$9,000	$10,500	$12,000
Less: depreciation	2,800	700	700	700	700
Cash requirements	$36,700	$7,300	$8,300	$ 9,800	$11,300

Now comes the all important cash budget. You put it together by using the Collection of Accounts Receivable Budget; Selling Expenses Budget—Cash Requirements; Administrative Expenses Budget—Cash Requirements; Payment of Purchases Budget; Direct Labor Budget—Cash Requirements; and Manufacturing Budget—Cash Requirements.

Take $15,000 as the beginning balance, and assume that dividends of $20,000 are to be paid in the fourth quarter.

Cash Budget
For the Year Ended December 31, 19 ____

	Total	1st Quarter	2nd Quarter	3rd Quarter	4th Quarter
Beginning cash balance.......	$ 15,000	$15,000	$ 3,850	$ 13,300	$ 25,750
Cash collections.............	361,950	69,000	82,800	97,6500	112,500
Total....................	$376,950	$84,000	$86,650	$110,950	$138,250
Cash payments					
Purchases................	$ 58,625	$11,750	$13,875	$ 15,375	$ 17,625
Direct labor	98,750	20,000	22,500	26,250	30,000
Mfg. overhead............	38,700	7,300	8,300	9,800	11,300
Selling expense	91,600	17,275	21,025	24,775	28,525
Adm. expenses..............	33,300	6,300	7,650	9,000	10,350
Federal income tax........	27,525	27,525			
Dividends	20,000				20,000
Interest expenses	450				450
Loan repayment	10,000				10,000
Total...................	$376,950	$90,150	$73,350	$ 85,200	$128,250
Cash deficiency...........		($6,150)			
Bank loan received.........	10,000	10,000			
Ending cash balance	$ 10,000	$ 3,850	$13,300	$ 25,750	$ 10,000

Now you are ready to **prepare a budget balance sheet**. Take the account balances of last year and combine them with the transactions reflected in the various budgets you have compiled. You will come out with a sheet resembling this:

Budgeted Balance Sheet
December 31, 19 ____
Assets

	19 ____	19 ____
Current assets:		
Cash..	$ 10,000	$ 15,000
Accounts receivable...............................	11,500	6,666
Less: allowance for doubtful accounts..............	(1,150)	(666)
Inventory:		
Raw materials.................................	6,750	3,000
Finished goods................................	22,500	10,000
Total current assets	$ 49,600	34,000
Fixed assets:		
Land..	$ 50,000	$ 50,000
Building..	148,000	148,000
Less: allowance for depreciation..................	(37,000)	(33,000)
Total fixed assets............................	$161,100	$164,700
Total assets	$210,600	$198,700

Liabilities and Shareholders' Equity

	19 ____	19 ____
Current liabilities:		
Account payable.................................	$ 9,375	$ 5,000
Shareholders' equity:		
Capital stock (10,000 shares; $10 par value)........	$100,000	$110,000
Retained earnings...............................	101,225	93,700
	$201,225	$193,700
Total liabilities and shareholders' equity..............	$210,600	$198,700

In order to make the most effective use of your budgets to plan profits, you will want to establish reporting devices. Throughout the time span you have set, you need periodic reports and reviews on both efforts and accomplishments. These let you know whether your budget plan is being attained and help you keep control throughout the process. It is through comparing actual performance with budgeted projections that you maintain control of the operations.

Your company should be structured along functional lines, with well identified areas of responsibility and authority. Then, depending upon the size of your company, the budget reports can be prepared to correspond with the organizational structure of the company.

Two typical budget reports* are shown below to demonstrate various forms these reports may take.

Report of Actual and Budgeted Sales
For the Year Ended December 31, 19 ____

| | Actual sales | Budgeted sales | Variations from budget (under) | |
			Quarterly	Cumulative
1st Quarter	$	$	$	$
2nd Quarter				
3rd Quarter				
4th Quarter				

Budgeted Report on Selling Expenses
For the Year Ended December 31, 19 ____

Budget This Month	Actual This Month	Variation This Month	Budget Year to Date	Actual Year to Date	Variations Year to Date	Remarks

*SBMS 15, SBA's *Handbook of Small Business Finance*, Chapter 4, contains an excellent explanation of how to prepare the Cash Flow Budget. You may also want to contact your banker to request a form distributed by Robert Morris Associates designed for use on a month-to-month basis in preparing this Budget.

Remember, the Cash Flow Statement used as the business's Budget allows the owner/manager to anticipate problems rather than react to them after they occur. It permits comparison of actual receipts and disbursements against projections to identify errors in the forecast. If cash flow is analyzed monthly, the manager can correct the cause of the error before it harms profitability.

VI. Pricing Policy

Identifying the actual cost of doing business requires careful and accurate analysis. No one is expected to calculate the cost of doing business with complete accuracy. However, failure to calculate all actual costs properly to ensure an adequate profit margin is a frequent and often overlooked cause of business failure.

Establishing Selling Prices

The costs of raw materials, labor, indirect overhead, and research and development must be carefully studied *before* setting the selling price of items offered by your business. These factors must be regularly re-evaluated, as costs fluctuate.

Regardless of the strategies employed to maximize profitability, the method of costing products offered for resale is basic. It involves four major categories:

• Direct Material Costs

- Direct Labor Costs

- Overhead Expenses

- Profit Desired

Combining these factors allows you to calculate an item's minimum sales price, which is described below:

1. **Calculate your Direct Material Costs.** Direct material costs are the total cost of all raw materials used to produce the item for sale. Divide this total cost by the number of items produced from these raw materials to derive the Total Direct Materials Cost Per Item.

2. **Calculate your Direct Labor Costs.** Direct labor costs are the wages paid to employees to produce the item. Divide this total direct labor cost by the total number of items produced to get the Total Direct Labor Cost Per Item.

3. **Calculate your Total Overhead Expenses.** Overhead expenses include rent, gas and electricity, telephone, packing and shipping, delivery and freight charges, cleaning expenses, insurance, office supplies, postage, repairs and maintenance, and the manager's salary. In other words, all operating expenses incurred during the same time period that you used for calculating the costs above (one year, one quarter, or one month). Divide the Total Overhead Expense by the number of items produced for sale during that same time period to get the Total Overhead Expense Per Item.

4. **Calculate Total Cost Per Item.** Add the Total Direct Material Cost Per Item, the Total Direct Labor Cost Per Item, and the Total Overhead Expense Per Item to derive the Total Cost Per Item.

5. **Calculate the Profit Per Item.** Now, calculate the profit you determine appropriate for each category of item offered for sale based on the sales and profit strategy you have set for your

business.

6. Calculate the Total Price Per Item. Add the Profit Figure Per Item to the Total Cost Per Item.

A Pricing Example

You produce skirts that take 1 1/2 yards of fabric per skirt, and you can manufacture three skirts per day. The fabric costs $2.00 per yard. The normal work week is five days. If you complete three skirts per day, your week's production is 15 skirts.

1. Calculate Direct Materials Cost

Materials	*Cost*
Fabric for 1 week's production: 15 skirts x 1 1/2 yds. each = 22 1/2 yds. x $2 per yd.	$45.00
Linings, interfacings, etc.: $.50 per skirt x 15 skirts	7.50
Zippers, buttons, snaps: $.50 per skirt x 15 skirts	7.50
Belts, ornaments, etc.: $.75 per skirt x 15 skirts	11.25
Thread, seam binding, etc.: One week's supply	5.00
Total Direct Materials Cost:	**$76.25 per week**

$$\frac{\text{Total Direct Materials Cost per week}}{\text{15 skirts per week}} = \$5.08 \text{ Direct Materials Cost per skirt}$$

2. Calculate Direct Labor Costs

Wages paid to employees = $100.00 per week

$$\frac{\text{Total Direct Labor Cost per week}}{\text{15 skirts}} = \$6.67 \text{ Direct Labor Cost per skirt}$$

3. Calculate Overhead Expenses Per Month

Overhead Expenses	Monthly Expenses
Owner's Salary	$400.00
Rent	100.00
Electricity	24.00
Telephone	12.00
Insurance	15.00
Cleaning	20.00
Packing Materials and Supplies	15.00
Delivery and Freight	20.00
Office Supplies, Postage	10.00
Repairs and Maintenance	15.00
Payroll Taxes	5.00
Total Monthly Overhead Expenses:	$636.00

15 skirts per week x 4 weeks in one month = 60 skirts per month.

$$\frac{\text{Total Monthly Overhead Expenses}}{\text{60 skirts per month}} = \$10.60 \text{ Overhead Cost per skirt}$$

4. Calculate the Total Cost per Skirt by adding the total individual costs per skirt calculated in the three preceding steps.

Total Direct Material Cost per Skirt	$5.08
Total Direct Labor Cost per Skirt	6.67
Total Overhead Expense per Skirt	10.60
TOTAL COST PER SKIRT	$22.35

5. Assume you want to make a profit of $5.00 per skirt.

6. Calculate the Total Price Per Item:

50

Total Cost per Skirt	$22.35
Total Profit per Skirt	5.00
Total Selling Price Per Skirt	$27.35

The Retailer's Mark-Up

A word of caution is in order regarding the popular but misunderstood pricing method known as retailers mark-up. Retail mark-up means the amount added to the price of an item to arrive at the retail sales price, either in dollars or as a percentage of the cost.

For example, if a single item costing $8.00 is sold for $12.00 it carries a mark-up of $4.00 or 50 percent. If a group of items costing $6,000 is offered for $10,000, the mark-up is $4,000 or 66 2/3 percent. While in these illustrations the mark-up percentage appears generally to equal the gross margin percentages, the mark-up is **not** the same as the gross margin. Adding mark-up to the price merely to simplify pricing will almost always adversely affect profitability.

To demonstrate, assume a manager determines from past records that the business's operating expenses average 29 percent of sales. She decides that she is entitled to a profit of 3 percent. So she prices her goods at a 32 percent gross margin, in order to earn a 3 percent profit after all operating expenses are paid. What she fails to realize, however, is that once the goods are displayed, some may be lost through pilferage. Others may have to be marked down later in order to sell them, or employees may purchase some of them at a discount. Therefore, the total reductions (mark-downs, shortages, discounts) in the sales price realized from selling all the inventory actually add up to an annual average of six percent of total sales. To correctly calculate the necessary mark-up required to yield a 32 percent gross margin, these reductions to inventory must be anticipated and added into its selling price. Using the formula:

$$\text{Initial Mark-up} = \frac{\text{Desired Gross Margin} + \text{Retail Reductions}}{100\text{ Percent} + \text{Retail Reductions}}$$

$$\frac{32\text{ percent} + 6\text{ percent}}{100\text{ percent} + 6\text{ percent}} = \frac{38\text{ percent}}{106\text{ percent}} = 35.85\text{ percent}$$

To obtain the desired gross margin of 32 percent, therefore, the retailer must initially mark up his inventory by nearly 36 percent.

Pricing Policies and Profitability Goals

Break-Even Analysis, discussed in Chapter IV, and Return on Investment, described in Chapter III, should be reviewed at this time. Remember, all costs (direct and indirect), the break-even point, desired profit, and the methods of calculating sales price from these factors must be thoroughly studied when you establish pricing policies and profitability goals. They should be understood before you offer items for sale because an omission or error in these calculations could make the difference between success and failure.

Selling Strategy
Proper product pricing is only one facet of overall planning for profitability. A second major factor to be determined once costs, break-even point, and profitability goals have been analyzed, is the selling strategy. Three sales planning approaches are used (often concurrently) by businesses to develop final pricing policies, as

52

they strive to compete successfully.

In the first, employed as a short-term strategy in the earliest stages of a business, the owner/manager sells products at such low prices that the business only breaks even (no profit), while trying to attract future steady customers. As volume grows, the owner/manager gradually builds in the profit margin necessary to achieve the targeted Return on Investment.

"Loss leaders" are a second strategy practiced in both developing and mature business. While a few items are sold at a loss, most goods are priced for healthy profits. The hope is that while customers are in the store to purchase the low-price items, they will also buy enough other goods to make the seller's overall profitability higher than if he had not used "come-ons." The seller wants to maximize total profit and can sacrifice profit on a few items to achieve that goal.

The third strategy recognizes that maximum profit does not result only from selling goods at relatively high profit margins. The relationship of volume, price, cost of merchandise, and operational expenses determines profitability. Price increases may result in fewer sales and decreased profits. Reductions in prices, if sales volume is substantially increased, may produce satisfactory profits.

There is no arbitrary rule about this. It is perfectly possible for two stores, with different pricing structures to exist side by side and both be successful. It is the owner/manager's responsibility to identify and understand the market factors that affect his or her unique business circumstances. The level of service (delivery, availability of credit, store hours, product advice, and the like) may permit a business to charge higher prices in order to cover the costs of such services. Location, too, often permits a business to charge more, since customers are often willing to pay a premium for convenience.

The point is that many considerations go into setting selling prices. Some small businesses do not seek to compete on price at all, finding an un- or under-occupied market niche, which can be a more certain path to success. What is important is that all factors that affect pricing must be recognized and analyzed for their costs as well as their benefits.

VII. Forecasting and Obtaining Capital

Forecasting the need for capital, whether debt or equity, has already been discussed in Chapter V. This chapter looks at the types and uses of external capital and the usual sources of such capital.

Types and Sources of Capital

The capital to finance a business has two major forms: debt and equity. Creditor money (debt) comes from trade credit, loans made by financial institutions, leasing companies, and customers who have made prepayments on larger—frequently manufactured—orders. Equity is money received by the company in exchange for some portion of ownership. Sources include the entrepreneur's own money; money from family, friends, or other non-professional investors; or money from venture capitalists, Small Business Investment Companies (SBICs), and Minority Enterprise Small Business Investment Companies (MESBICs) both funded by the SBA.

Debt capital, depending upon its sources (e.g., trade, bank, leasing company, mortgage company) comes into the business for short or intermediate periods. Owner or equity capital remains in the company for the life of the business (unless replaced by other equity) and is repaid only when and if there is a surplus at liquidation of the business—**after** all creditors are repaid.

Acquiring such funds depends entirely on the business's ability to repay with interest (debt) or appreciation (equity). Financial performance (reflected in the Financial Statements discussed in Chapter II) and realistic, thorough management planning and control (shown by Pro Formas and Cash Flow Budgets), are the determining factors in whether or not a business can attract the debt and equity funding it needs to operate and expand.

Business capital can be further classified as equity capital, working capital, and growth capital. *Equity capital* is the cornerstone of the financial structure of any company. As you will recall from Chapter II, equity is technically the part of the Balance Sheet reflecting the ownership of the company. It represents the total value of the business, all other financing being debt that must be repaid. Usually, you cannot get equity capital— at least not during the early stages of business growth.

Working capital is required to meet the continuing operational needs of the business, such as "carrying" accounts receivable, purchasing inventory, and meeting the payroll. In most businesses, these needs vary during the year, depending on activities (inventory build-up, seasonal hiring or layoffs, etc.) during the business cycle.

Growth capital is not directly related to cyclical aspects of the business. Growth capital is required when the business is expanding or being altered in some significant and costly way that is expected to result in higher and increased cash flow. Lenders of growth capital frequently depend on anticipated increased profit for repayment over an extended period of time, rather than expecting to be repaid from seasonal increases in liquidity as is the case of working capital lenders.

Every growing business needs all three types: equity, working, and growth capital. You should not expect a single financing program maintained for a short period of time to eliminate future needs for additional capital.

As lenders and investors analyze the requirements of your business, they will distinguish between the three types of capital in the following way: 1) fluctuating needs (working capital); 2) needs to be repaid with profits over a period of a few years (growth capital); and 3) permanent needs (equity capital).

If you are asking for a working capital loan, you will be expected to show how the loan can be repaid through cash (liquidity) during the business's next full operating cycle, generally a one year cycle. If you seek growth capital, you will be expected to show how the capital will be used to increase your business enough to be able to repay the loan within several years (usually not more than seven). If you seek equity capital, it must be raised from investors who will take the risk for dividend returns or capital gains, or a specific share of the business.

Borrowing Working Capital

Chapter II defined working capital as the difference between current assets and current liabilities. To the extent that a business does not generate enough money to pay trade debt as it comes due, this cash must be borrowed.

Commercial banks obviously are the largest source of such loans, which have the following characteristics: 1) The loans are short-term but renewable; 2) they may fluctuate according to seasonal needs or follow a fixed schedule of repayment (amortization); 3) they require periodic full repayment ("clean up"); 4) they are granted primarily only when the ratio of net current assets comfortably exceeds net current liabilities; and 5) they are sometimes unsecured but more often secured by current assets (e.g., accounts receivable and inventory). Advances can usually be obtained for as much as 70 to 80 percent of quality (likely to be paid) receivables and to 40 to 50 percent of inventory. Banks grant unsecured credit only when they feel the general liquidity and overall financial strength of a business provide assurance for repayment of the loan.

You may be able to predict a specific interval, say three to five months, for which you need financing. A bank may then agree to issue credit for a specific term. Most likely, you will need working capital to finance outflow peaks in your business cycle. Working capital then supplements equity. Most working capital credits are established on a one-year basis.

Although most unsecured loans fall into the one-year line of credit category, another frequently used type, the amortizing loan, calls for a fixed program of reduction, usually on a monthly or quarterly basis. For such loans your bank is likely to agree to terms longer than a year, as long as you continue to meet the principal reduction schedule.

It is important to note that while a loan from a bank for working capital can be negotiated only for a relatively short term, satisfactory performance can allow the arrangement to be continued indefinitely.

Most banks will expect you to pay off your loans once a year (particularly if they are unsecured) in perhaps 30 or 60 days. This is known as "the annual clean up," and it should occur when the business has the greatest liquidity. This debt reduction normally follows a seasonal sales peak when inventories have been reduced and most receivables have been collected.

You may discover that it becomes progressively more difficult to repay debt or "clean up" within the specified time. This difficulty usually occurs because: 1) Your business is growing and its current activity represents a considerable increase over the corresponding period of the previous year; 2) you have increased your short-term capital requirement because of new promotional programs or additional operations; or 3) you are experiencing a temporary reduction in profitability and cash flow.

Frequently, such a condition justifies obtaining both working capital and amortizing loans. For example, you might try to arrange a combination of a $15,000 open line of credit to handle peak financial requirements during the business cycle and $20,000 in amortizing loans to be repaid at, say $4,000 per quarter. In appraising such a request, a commercial bank will insist on justification based on past experience and future projections. The bank will want to know: How the $15,000 line of credit will be self-liquidating during the year (with ample room for the annual clean up); and how your business will produce increased profits and resulting cash flow to meet the schedule of amortization on the $20,000 portion in spite of increasing your business's interest expense.

Borrowing Growth Capital

Lenders expect working capital loans to be repaid through cash generated in the short-term operations of the business, such as, selling goods or services and collecting receivables. Liquidity rather than overall profitability supports such borrowing programs. Growth capital loans are usually scheduled to be repaid over longer periods with profits from business activities extending several years into the future. Growth capital loans are, therefore, secured by collateral such as machinery and equipment, fixed assets which guarantee that lenders will recover their money should the business be unable to make repayment.

59

For a growth capital loan you will need to demonstrate that the growth capital will be used to increase your cash flow through increased sales, cost savings, and/or more efficient production. Although your building, equipment, or machinery will probably be your collateral for growth capital funds, you will also be able to use them for general business purposes, so long as the activity you use them for promises success. Even if you borrow only to acquire a single piece of new equipment, the lender is likely to insist that all your machinery and equipment be pledged.

Instead of bank financing a particular piece of new equipment, it may be possible to arrange a lease. You will not actually own the equipment, but you will have exclusive use of it over a specified period. Such an arrangement usually has tax advantages. It lets you use funds that would be tied up in the equipment, if you had purchased it. It also affords the opportunity to make sure the equipment meets your needs before you purchase it.

Major equipment may also be purchased on a time payment plan, sometimes called a Conditional Sales Purchase. Ownership of the property is retained by the seller until the buyer has made all the payments required by the contract. (Remember, however, that time payment purchases usually require substantial down payments and even leases require cash advances for several months of lease payments.)

Long-term growth capital loans for more than five but less than fifteen years are also obtainable. Real estate financing with repayment over many years on an established schedule is the best example. The loan is secured by the land and/or buildings the money was used to buy. Most businesses are best financed by a combination of these various credit arrangements.

When you go to a bank to request a loan, you must be prepared to present your company's case persuasively. You should bring your financial plan consisting of a Cash Budget for the next twelve months, Pro Forma Balance Sheets, and Income Statements for the next three to five years. You should be able to explain and amplify these statements and the underlying assumptions on which the figures are based. Obviously, your assumptions must be convincing and your projections supportable. Finally, many banks prefer statements audited by an outside accountant with the accountant's signed opinion that the statements were prepared in accordance with generally accepted accounting principles and that they fairly present the financial condition of your business.

If borrowing growth capital is necessary and no private conventional source can be found, the U.S. Small Business Administration (SBA) may be able to guarantee up to 90 percent of a local bank loan. By law, SBA cannot consider a loan application without evidence that the loan could not be obtained elsewhere on reasonable terms without SBA assistance. Even for such guaranteed loans, however, the borrower must demonstrate the ability to repay.

Borrowing Permanent Equity Capital

Permanent capital sometimes comes from sources other than the business owner/manager. Considered ownership contributions, they are different from "stockholders equity" in the traditional sense of the phrase. Small Business Investment Companies (SBIC's) licensed and financed by the Small Business Administration are authorized to provide venture capital to small business concerns. This captital may be in the form of secured and/or unsecured loans or debt securities represented by common and preferred stock.

Venture capital, another source of equity capital, is extremely difficult to define; however, it is high risk capital offered with the principal objective of earning capital gains for the investor. While venture capitalists are usually prepared to wait longer than the average investor for a profitable return, they usually expect in excess of 15 percent return on their investment. Often they expect to take an active part in determining the objectives of the business. These investors may also assist the small business owner/manager by providing experienced guidance in marketing, product ideas, and additional financing alternatives as the business develops. Even though turning to venture capital may create more bosses, their advice could be as valuable as the money they lend. Be aware, however, that venture capitalists are looking for businesses with real potential for growth and for future sales in the millions of dollars.

Figure 7-1

Financing Sources for Your Business

Equity (Sell part of company)
- Family, friends, and other non-professional investors
- Venture Capitalists
- Small Business Investment Companies (SBICs and MESBICs)

Personal Loans
- Banks
  - —Unsecured loans (rare)
  - —Loans secured by:
    Real Estate
    Stocks and Bonds
- Finance Companies
  - —Loans secured by:
    Real Estate
    Personal Assets
- Credit Unions
  - —Unsecured "signature" loans
  - —Loans secured by:
    Real Estate (some credit unions)
    Personal Assets
- Savings and Loan Associations
  - —Unsecured loans (rare)
  - —Loans secured by Real Estate
- Mortgage Brokers and Private Investors
  - —Loans secured by Real Estate
- Life Insurance Companies
  - —Policy loans (borrow against cash value)

Business Loans

Loans

- Banks (short-term)
  - —Unsecured loans (for established,
    financially sound companies only)

—Loans secured by:
  Accounts Receivable
  Inventory
  Equipment
Banks (long-term)
 —Loans secured by:
  Real Estate
 —Loans guaranteed by:
  Small Business Administration (SBA)
  Farmers Home Administration (FmHA)
• Commercial Finance Companies
 —Loans secured by:
  Real Estate
  Equipment
  Inventory
  Accounts Receivable
• Life Insurance Companies
 —Loans secured by commercial Real Estate
  (worth at least $150,000)
• Small Business Administration (SBA)
 —Loans secured by:
  All available business assets
  All available personal assets
• Suppliers
 —Trade Credit
• Customers
 —Prepayment on orders

Leasing

• Banks
• Leasing Companies
 —Loans secured by:
  Equipment
Sales of Receivables (called "factoring")

(Source: The Business Store, Santa Rosa, California.)

64

Applying for Capital

Below is the minimum information you must make available to lenders and investors:

1. *Discussion of the Business*
   - Name, address, and telephone number.
   - Type of business you are in now or want to expand or start.

2. *Amount of Money You Need to Borrow*
   - Ask for *all* you will need. Don't ask for a part of the total and think you can come back for more later. This could indicate to the lender that you are a poor planner.

3. *How You Will Use the Money*
   - List each way the borrowed money will be used.
   - Itemize the amount of money required for each purpose.

4. *Proposed Terms of the Loan*
   - Include a payback schedule. Even though the lender has the final say in setting the terms of the loan, if you suggest terms, you will retain a negotiating position.

5. *Financial Support Documents*
   - Show where the money will come from to repay the loan through the following projected statements:

   —Profit and Loss Statements (one year for working capital loan requests and three to five years for growth capital requests)
   —Cash Flow Statements (one year for working capital loan requests and three to five years for growth capital requests)

6. *Financial History of the Business*
   - Include the following financial statements for the last three years:
      —Balance Sheet
      —Profit and Loss Statement

—Accounts Receivable and Accounts Payable Listings and Agings

7. *Personal Financial Statement of the Owner(s)*
   - Personal Assets and Liabilities
   - Resume(s)

8. *Other Useful Information Includes*
   - Letters of Intent from Prospective Customers
   - Leases or Buy/Sell Agreements Affecting Your Business
   - Reference Letters

Although it is not required, it is useful to calculate the ratios described in Chapter III for your business over the past three years. Use this information to prove the strong financial health and good trends in your business's development and to demonstrate that you use such management tools to plan and control your business's growth.

VIII. Financial Management Planning

Studies overwhelmingly identify bad management as the leading cause of business failure. Bad management translates to poor planning by management.

All too often, the owner is so caught up in the day-to-day tasks of getting the product out the door and struggling to collect receivables to meet the payroll that he or she does not plan. There never seems to be time to prepare Pro Formas or Budgets. Often new managers understand their products but not the financial statements or the bookkeeping records, which they feel are for the benefit of the IRS or the bank. Such overburdened owner/-managers can scarcely identify what will affect their businesses next week, let alone over the coming months and years. But, you may ask, "What should I do? How can I, as a small business owner/manager, avoid getting bogged down? How can I ensure success?"

Success may be ensured only by focusing on all factors affecting a business's performance. Focusing on planning is essential to survival.

Short-term planning is generally concerned with profit planning or budgeting. Long-term planning is generally strategic, setting goals for sales growth and profitability over a minimum of three to five years.

The tools for short- and long-term plans have been explained in the previous chapters: Pro Forma Income Statements, Cash Flow Statements or Budgets, Ratio Analysis, and pricing considerations. The business's short-term plan should be prepared on a monthly basis for a year into the future, employing the Pro Forma Income Statement and the Cash Flow Budget.

Long-Term Planning

The long-term or strategic plan focuses on Pro Forma Statements of Income prepared for annual periods three to five years into the future. You may be asking yourself, "How can I possibly predict what will affect my business that far into the future?" Granted, it's hard to imagine all the variables that will affect your business in the next year, let alone the next three to five years. The key, however, is control—control of your business's future course of expansion through the use of the financial tools explained in the preceding chapters.

First determine a rate of growth that is desirable and reasonably attainable. Then employ Pro Formas and Cash Flow Budgets to calculate the capital required to finance the inventory, plant, equipment, and personnel needs necessary to attain that growth in sales volume. The business owner/manager must anticipate capital needs in time to make satisfactory arrangements for outside funds if internally generated funds from retained earnings are insufficient.

Growth can be funded in only two ways: with profits or by borrowing. If expansion outstrips the capital available to support

68

higher levels of accounts receivable, inventory, fixed assets, and operating expenses, a business's development will be slowed or stopped entirely by its failure to meet debts as they become payable. Such insolvency will result in the business's assets being liquidated to meet the demands of the creditors. The only way to avoid this "outstripping of capital" is by planning to control growth. *Growth must be understood to be controlled.* This understanding requires knowledge of past financial performance and of the future requirements of the business.

These needs must be forecast in writing—using the Pro Forma Income Statement in particular—for three to five years in the future. After projecting reasonable sales volumes and profitability, use the Cash Flow Budget to determine (on a quarterly basis for the next three to five years) how these projected sales volumes translate into the flow of cash in and out of the business during normal operations. Where additional inventory, equipment, or other physical assets are necessary to support the sales forecast, you must determine whether or not the business will generate enough profit to sustain the growth forecast.

Often, businesses simply grow too rapidly for internally generated cash to sufficiently support the growth. If profits are inadequate to carry the growth forecast, the owner/manager must either make arrangements for working growth capital to borrowed, or slow growth to allow internal cash to "catch up" and keep pace with the expansion. Because arranging financing and obtaining additional equity capital takes time, this need must be anticipated well in advance to avoid business interruption.

To develop effective long-term plans, you should do the following steps:

1. **Determine your personal objectives and how they affect your willingness and ability to pursue financial goals for your business.** This consideration, often overlooked, will help you determine whether or not your business goals fit your personal

plans. For example, suppose you hope to become a millionaire by age 45 through your business but your long-term strategic plan reveals that only modest sales growth and very slim profit margins on that volume are attainable in your industry. You must either adjust your personal goals or get into a different business. Long-range planning enables you to be realistic about the future of your personal and business expectations.

2. **Set goals and objectives for the company (growth rates, return on investment, and direction as the business expands and matures).** Express these goals in specific numbers, for example, sales growth of 10 percent a year, increases in gross and net profit margins of 2 to 3 percent a year, a return on investment of not less than 9 to 10 percent a year. Use these long-range plans to develop forecasts of sales and profitability and compare actual results from operations to these forecasts. If after these goals are established actual performance continuously falls short of target, the wise business owner will reassess both the realism of expectations and the desirability of continuing to pursue the enterprise.

3. **Develop long-range plans that enable you to attain your goals and objectives.** Focus on the strengths and weaknesses of your business and on internal and external factors that will affect the accomplishment of your goals. Develop strategies based upon careful analysis of all relevant factors (pricing strategies, market potential, competition, cost of borrowed and equity capital as compared to using only profits for expansions, etc.) to provide direction for the future of your business.

4. **Focus on the financial, human, and physical requirements necessary to fulfill your plan by developing forecasts of sales, expenses, and retain earnings over the next three to five years.**

5. **Study methods of operation, product mix, new market opportunities, and other such factors to help identify ways to improve your company's productivity and profitability.**

6. **Revise, revise.** Always use your most recent financial statements to adjust your short- and long-term plans. Compare your company's financial performance regularly with current industry data to determine how your results compare with others in your industry. Learn where your business may have performance weaknesses. Don't be afraid to modify your plans if your expectations have been either too aggressive or too conservative.

Planning is a perpetual process. It is the key to prosperity for your business.

BASIC FUNDAMENTALS OF A FINANCIAL STATEMENT

TABLE OF CONTENTS

BASIC FUNDAMENTALS
OF A FINANCIAL STATEMENT

COMMENTARY

The ability to read and understand a financial statement is a basic requirement for the accountant, auditor, account clerk, bookkeeper, bank examiner. budget examiner, and, of course, for the executive who must manage and administer departmental affairs.

FINANCIAL REPORTS

Are financial reports really as difficult as all that? Well, if you know they are not so difficult because you have worked with them before, this section will be of auxiliary help for you. However, if you find financial statements a bit murky, but realize their great importance to you, we ought to get along fine together. For "mathematics," all we'll use is fourth-grade arithmetic.

Accountants, like all other professionals, have developed a specialized vocabulary. Sometimes this is helpful and sometimes plain confusing (like their practice of calling the income account, "Statement of Profit and Loss," when it is bound to be one or the other). But there are really only a score or so technical terms that you will have to get straight in mind. After that is done, the whole foggy business will begin to clear and in no time at all you'll be able to talk as wisely as the next fellow.

BALANCE SHEET

Look at the sample balance sheet printed on page 2, and we'll have an insight into how it is put together. This particular report is neither the simplest that could be issued, nor the most complicated. It is a good average sample of the kind of report issued by an up-to-date manufacturing company.

Note particularly that the *balance sheet* represents the situation as it stood on one particular day, December 31, not the record of a year's operation. This balance sheet is broken into two parts: on the left are shown *ASSETS* and on the right *LIABILITIES.* Under the asset column, you will find listed the value of things the company owns or are owed to the company. Under liabilities, are listed the things the company owes to others, plus reserves, surplus, and the stated value of the stockholders' interest in the company.

One frequently hears the comment, "Well, I don't see what a good balance sheet is anyway, because the assets and liabilities are always the same whether the company is successful or not."

It is true that they always balance and, by itself, a balance sheet doesn't tell much until it is analyzed. Fortunately, we can make a balance sheet tell its story without too much effort -- often an extremely revealing story, particularly, if we compare the records of several years. ASSETS The first notation on the asset side of the balance sheet is *CURRENT* ASSETS (item 1). In general, current assets include cash and things that can be turned into cash in a hurry, or that, in the normal course of business, will be turned into cash in the reasonably near future, usually within a year.

Item 2 on our sample sheet is *CASH.* Cash is just what you would expect -bills and silver in the till and money on deposit in the bank.

UNITED STATES GOVERNMENT SECURITIES is item 3. The general practice is to show securities listed as current assets at cost or market value, whichever is lower. The figure, for all reasonable purposes, represents the amount by which total cash could be easily increased if the company wanted to sell these securities.

The next entry is *ACCOUNTS RECEIVABLE* (item 4). Here we find the total amount of money owed to the company by its regular business creditors and collectable within the next year. Most of the money is owed to the company by its customers for goods that the company delivered on credit. If this were a department store instead of a manufacturer, what you owed the store on your charge account would be included here. Because some people fail to pay their bills, the company sets up a reserve for doubtful accounts, which it subtracts from all the money owed.

THE ABC MANUFACTURING COMPANY, INC.
CONSOLIDATED BALANCE SHEET – DECEMBER 31

Item			
1. CURRENT ASSETS			
2. Cash			
3. U.S. Government Securities			
4. Accounts Receivable (less reserves)		2,000,000	
5. Inventories (at lower of cost or market)		2,000,000	
6. Total Current Assets		$7,000,000	
7. INVESTMENT IN AFFIL-IATED COMPANY Not consolidated (at cost, not in excess of net assets)		200,000	
8. OTHER INVESTMENTS At cost, less than market		100,000	
9. PLANT IMPROVEMENT FUND		550,000	
10. PROPERTY, PLANT AND EQUIPMENT: Cost	$8,000,000		
11. Less Reserve for Depreciation	5,000,000		
12. NET PROPERTY		3,000,000	
13. PREPAYMENTS		50,000	
14. DEFERRED CHARGES		100,000	
15. PATENTS AND GOODWILL		100,000	
TOTAL		$11,100,000	

Item			
16. CURRENT LIABILITIES			
17. Accts. Payable		$ 300,000	
18. Accrued Taxes		800,000	
19. Accrued Wages, Interest and Other Expenses		370,000	
20. Total Current Liabilities		$1,470,000	
21. FIRST MORTGAGE SINK-ING FUND BONDS, 3 1/2% DUE 2002		2,000,000	
22. RESERVE FOR CON-TINGENCIES		200,000	
23. CAPITAL STOCK:			
24. 5% Preferred Stock (authorized and issued 10,000 shares of $100 par value)		$1,000,000	
25. Common stock (authorized and issued 400,000 shares of no par value)		1,000,000	
			2,000,000
26. SURPLUS:			
27. Earned		3,530,000	
28. Capital (arising from sale of common capital stock at price in excess of stated value)		1,900,000	
			5,430,000
TOTAL			$11,100,000

Item 5, *INVENTORIES,* is the value the company places on the supplies it owns. The inventory of a manufacturer may contain raw materials that it uses in making the things it sells, partially finished goods in process of manufacture and, finally, completed merchandise that it is ready to sell. Several methods are used to arrive at the value placed on these various items. The most common is to value them at their cost or present market value, whichever is lower. You can be reasonably confident, however, that the figure given is an honest and significant one for the particular industry if the report is certified by a reputable firm of public accountants.

Next on the asset side is *TOTAL CURRENT ASSETS* (item 6). This is an extremely important figure when used in connection with other items in the report, which we will come to presently. Then we will discover how to make total current assets tell their story.

INVESTMENT IN AFFILIATED COMPANY (item 7) represents the cost to our parent company of the capital stock of its *subsidiary* or affiliated company. A subsidiary is simply one company that is controlled by another. Most corporations that own other companies outright, lump the figures in a *CONSOLIDATED BALANCE SHEET.* This means that, under cash, for example, one would find a total figure that represented *all* of the cash of the parent company and of its wholly owned subsidiary. This is a perfectly reasonable procedure because, in the last analysis, all of the money is controlled by the same persons.

Our typical company shows that it has *OTHER INVESTMENTS* (item 8), in addition to its affiliated company. Sometimes good marketable securities other than Government bonds are carried as current assets, but the more conservative practice is to list these other security holdings separately. If they have been bought as a permanent investment, they would always be shown by themselves. "At cost, less than market" means that our company paid $100,000 for these other investments, but they are now worth more.

Among our assets is a *PLANT IMPROVEMENT FUND* (item 9). Of course, this item does not appear in all company balance sheets, but is typical of *special funds* that companies set up for one purpose or another. For example, money set aside to pay off part of the bonded debt of a company might be segregated into a special fund. The money our directors have put aside to improve the plant would often be invested in Government bonds.

FIXED ASSETS

The next item (10), is *PROPERTY, PLANT AND EQUIPMENT,* but it might just as well be labeled *Fixed Assets* as these terms are used more or less interchangeably. Under item 10, the report gives the value of land, buildings, and machinery and such movable things as trucks, furniture, and hand tools. Historically, probably more sins were committed against this balance sheet item than any other.

In olden days, cattlemen used to drive their stock to market in the city. It was a common trick to stop outside of town, spread out some salt for the cattle to make them thirsty and then let them drink all the water they could hold. When they were weighed for sale, the cattlemen would collect cash for the water the stock had drunk. Business buccaneers, taking the cue from their farmer friends, would often "write up" the value of their fixed assets. In other words, they would increase the value shown on the balance sheet, making the capital stock appear to be worth a lot more than it was. *Watered stock* proved a bad investment for most stockholders. The practice has, fortunately, been stopped, though it took major financial reorganizations to squeeze the water out of some securities.

The most common practice today is to list fixed assets at cost. Often, there is no ready market for most of the things that fall under this heading, so it is not possible to give market value. A good report will tell what is included under fixed assets and how it has been valued. If the value has been increased by *write-up* or decreased by *write-down,* a footnote explanation is usually given. A *write-up* might occur, for instance, if the value of real estate increased substantially. A *write-down* might follow the invention of a new machine that put an important part of the company's equipment out of date.

3

DEPRECIATION

Naturally, all of the fixed property of a company will wear out in time (except, of course, non-agricultural land). In recognition of this fact, companies set up a *RESERVE FOR DEPRECIATION* (item 11). If a truck costs $4,000 and is expected to last four years, it will be depreciated at the rate of $1,000 a year.

Two other terms also frequently occur in connection with depreciation -*depletion* and *obsolescence.* Companies may lump depreciation, depletion, and obsolescence under a single title, or list them separately.

Depletion is a term used primarily by mining and oil companies (or any of the so-called extractive industries). Depletion means exhaust or use up. As the oil or other natural resource is used up, a reserve is set up, to compensate for the natural wealth the company no longer owns. This reserve is set up in recognition of the fact that, as the company sells its natural product, it must get back not only the cost of extracting but also the original cost of the natural resource.

Obsolescence represents the loss in value because a piece of property has gone out of date before it wore out. Airplanes are modern examples of assets that tend to get behind the times long before the parts wear out. (Women and husbands will be familiar with the speed at which ladies' hats "obsolesce.")

In our sample balance sheet we have placed the reserve for depreciation under fixed assets and then subtracted, giving us *NET PROPERTY* (item 12), which we add into the asset column. Sometimes, companies put the reserve for depreciation in the liability column. As you can see, the effect is just the same whether it is *subtracted* from assets or *added* to liabilities.

The manufacturer, whose balance sheet we use, rents a New York showroom and pays his rent yearly, in advance. Consequently, he has listed under assets *PREPAYMENTS* (item 13). This is listed as an asset because he has paid for the use of the showroom, but has not yet received the benefit from its use. The use is something coming to the firm in the following year and, hence, is an asset. The dollar value of this asset will decrease by one-twelfth each month during the coming year.

DEFERRED CHARGES (item 14) represents a type of expenditure similar to prepayment. For example, our manufacturer brought out a new product last year, spending $100,000 introducing it to the market. As the benefit from this expenditure will be returned over months or even years to come, the manufacturer did not think it reasonable to charge the full expenditure against costs during the year. He has *deferred* the charges and will write them off gradually.

INTANGIBLES

The last entry in our asset column is *PATENTS AND GOODWILL* (item 15). If our company were a young one, set up to manufacture some new patented prod uct, it would probably carry its patents at a substantial figure. In fact, *intangibles* of both old and new companies are often of great but generally unmeasurable worth.

Company practice varies considerably in assigning value to intangibles. Procter & Gamble, despite the tremendous goodwill that has been built up for IVORY SOAP, has reduced all of its intangibles to the nominal $1. Some of the big cigarette companies, on the contrary, place a high dollar value on the goodwill their brand names enjoy. Companies that spend a good deal for research and the development of new products are more inclined than others to reflect this fact in the value assigned to patents, license agreements, etc.

LIABILITIES

The liability side of the balance sheet appears a little deceptive at first glance. Several of the entries simply don't sound like liabilities by any ordinary definition of the term.

The first term on the liability side of any balance sheet is usually *CURRENT LIABILITIES* (item 16). This is a companion to the *Current Assets* item across the page and includes all debts that fall due within the next year. The relation between current assets and current liabilities is one of the most revealing things to be gotten from the balance sheet, but we will go into that quite thoroughly later on.

ACCOUNTS PAYABLE (item 17) represents the money that the company owes to its ordinary business creditors -- unpaid bills for materials, supplies, insurance, and the like. Many companies itemize the money they owe in a much more detailed fashion than we have done, but, as you will see, the totals are the most interesting thing to us.

Item 18, *ACCRUED TAXES,* is the tax bill that the company estimates it still owes for the past year. We have lumped all taxes in our balance sheet, as many companies do. However, sometimes you will find each type of tax given separately. If the detailed procedure is followed, the description of the tax is usually quite sufficient to identify the separate items.

Accounts Payable was defined as the money the company owed to its regular business creditors. The company also owes, on any given day, wages to its own employees; interest to its bondholders and to banks from which it may have borrowed money; fees to its attorneys; pensions, etc. These are all totaled under *ACCRUED WAGES, INTEREST AND OTHER EXPENSES* (item 19).

TOTAL CURRENT LIABILITIES (item 20) is just the sum of everything that the company owed on December 31 and which must be paid sometime in the next twelve months.

It is quite clear that all of the things discussed above are liabilities. The rest of the entries on the liability side of the balance sheet, however, do not seem at first glance to be liabilities.

Our balance sheet shows that the company, on December 31, had $2,000,000 of 3 1/2 percent First Mortgage *BONDS* outstanding (item 21). Legally, the money received by a company when it sells bonds is considered a loan to the company. Therefore, it is obvious that the company owes to the bondholders an amount equal to the face value or the *call price* of the bonds it has outstanding. The call price is a figure usually larger than the face value of the bonds at which price the company can *call* the bonds in from the bondholders and pay them off before they ordinarily fall due. The date that often occurs as part of the name of a bond is the date at which the company has promised to pay off the loan from the bondholders.

RESERVES

The next heading, *RESERVE FOR CONTINGENCIES* (item 22), sounds more like an asset than a liability. "My reserves," you might say, "are dollars in the bank, and dollars in the bank are assets."

No one would deny that you have something there. In fact, the corporation treasurer also has his reserve for contingencies balanced by either cash or some kind of unspecified investment on the asset side of the ledger. His reason for setting up a reserve on the liability side of the balance sheet is a precaution against making his financial position seem better than it is. He decided that the company might have to pay out this money during the coming year if certain things happened. If he did not set up the "reserve," his surplus would appear larger by an amount equal to his reserve.

A very large reserve for contingencies or a sharp increase in this figure from the previous year should be examined closely by the investor. Often, in the past, companies tried to hide their true earnings by transferring funds into a contingency reserve. As a reserve looks somewhat like a true liability, stockholders were confused about the real value of their securities. When a reserve is not set up for protection against some very probable loss or expenditure, it should be considered by the investor as part of surplus.

CAPITAL STOCK

Below reserves there is a major heading, *CAPITAL STOCK* (item 23). Companies may have one type of security outstanding, or they may have a dozen. All of the issues that represent shares of ownership are capital, regardless of what they are called on the balance sheet -- preferred stock, preference stock, common stock, founders' shares, capital stock, or something else.

Our typical company has one issue of 5 per cent *PREFERRED STOCK* (item 24). It is called *preferred* because those who own it have a right to dividends and assets before the *common* stockholders -- that is, the holders are in a preferred position as owners. Usually, preferred stockholders do not have a voice in company affairs unless the company fails to pay them dividends at the promised rate. Their rights to dividends are almost always *cumulative.* This simply means that all past dividends must be paid before the other stockholders can receive anything. Preferred stockholders are not creditors of the company so it cannot properly be said that the company *owes* them the value of their holdings. However, in case the company decided to go out of business, preferred stockholders would have a prior claim on anything that was left in the company treasury after all of the creditors, including the bondholders, were paid off. In practice, this right does not always mean much, but it does explain why the book value of their holdings is carried as a liability.

COMMON STOCK (item 25) is simple enough as far as definition is concerned it represents the rights of the ordinary owner of the company. Each company has as many owners as it has stockholders. The proportion of the company that each stockholder owns is determined by the number of shares he has. However, neither the book value of a no-par common stock, nor the par value of an issue that has a given par, can be considered as representing either the original sale price, the market value, or what would be left for the stockholders if the company were liquidated.

A profitable company will seldom be dissolved. Once things have taken such a turn that dissolution appears desirable, the stated value of the stock is generally nothing but a fiction. Even if the company is profitable as a going institution, once it ceases to function even its tangible assets drop in value because there is not usually a ready market for its inventory of raw materials and semi-finished goods, or its plant and machinery.

SURPLUS

The last major heading on the liability side of the balance sheet is *SURPLUS* (item 26). The surplus, of course, is not a liability in the popular sense at all. It represents, on our balance sheet, the difference between the stated value of our common stock and the net assets behind the stock.

Two different kinds of surplus frequently appear on company balance sheets, and our company has both kinds. The first type listed is *EARNED* surplus (item 27). Earned surplus is roughly similar to your own savings. To the corporation, earned surplus is that part of net income which has not been paid to stockholders as dividends. It still *belongs* to you, but the directors have decided that it is best for the company and the stockholders to keep it in the business. The surplus may be invested in the plant just as you might invest part of your savings in your home. It may also be in cash or securities.

In addition to the earned surplus, our company also has a *CAPITAL* surplus (item 28) of $1,900.00, which the balance sheet explains arose from selling the stock at a higher cost per share than is given as its stated value. A little arithmetic shows that the stock is carried on the books at $2.50 a share while the capital surplus amounts to $4.75 a share. From this we know that the company actually received an average of $7.25 net a share for the stock when it was sold.

WHAT DOES THE BALANCE SHEET SHOW?

Before we undertake to analyze the balance sheet figures, a word on just what an investor can expect to learn is in order. A generation or more ago, before present accounting standards had gained wide acceptance, considerable imagination went into the preparation of balance sheets. This, naturally, made the public skeptical of financial reports. Today, there is no substantial ground for skepticism. The certified public accountant, the listing requirements of the national stock exchanges, and the regulations of the Securities and Exchange Commission have, for all practical purposes, removed the grounds for doubting the good faith of financial reports.

The investor, however, is still faced with the task of determining the significance of the figures. As we have already seen, a number of items are based, to a large degree, upon estimates, while others are, of necessity, somewhat arbitrary.

NET WORKING CAPITAL

There is one very important thing that we can find from the balance sheet and accept with the full confidence that we know what we are dealing with. That is net working capital, sometimes simply called working capital.

On the asset side of our balance sheet we have added up all of the current assets and show the total as item 6. On the liability side, item 20 gives the total of current liabilities. *Net working capital* or *net current assets* is the difference left after subtracting current liabilities from current assets. If you consider yourself an investor rather than a speculator, you should always insist that any company in which you invest have a comfortable amount of working capital. The ability of a company to meet its obligations with ease, expand its volume as business expands and take advantage of opportunities as they present themselves, is, to an important degree, determined by its working capital.

Probably the question in your mind is: *"Just what does 'comfortable amount' of working capital mean?"* Well, there are several methods used by analysts to judge whether a particular company has a sound working capital position. The first rough test for an industrial company is to compare the working capital figure with the current liability total. Most analysts say that minimum safety requires that net working capital at least equal current liabilities. Or, put another way, that current assets should be at least twice as large as current liabilities.

There are so many different kinds of companies, however, that this test requires a great deal of modification if it is to be really helpful in analyzing companies in different industries. To help you interpret the *current position* of a company in which you are considering investing, the *current ratio* is more helpful than the dollar total of working capital. The current ratio is current assets divided by current liabilities.

In addition to working capital and current ratio, there are two other ways of testing the adequacy of the current position. *Net quick assets* provide a rigorous and important test of a company's ability to meet its current obligations. Net quick assets are found by taking total current assets (item 6) and subtracting the value of inventories (item 5). A well-fixed industrial company should show a reasonable excess of quick assets over current liabilities..

Finally, many analysts say that a good industrial company should have at least as much working capital (current assets less current liabilities) as the total book value of its bonds and preferred stock. In other words, current liabilities, bonded debt, and preferred stock *altogether* should not exceed the current assets.

INVENTORY AND INVENTORY TURNOVER

In the recent past, there has been much talk of inventories. Many commentators have said that these carry a serious danger to company earnings if management allows them to increase too much. Of course, this has always been true, but present high prices have made everyone more inventory-conscious than usual.

There are several dangers in a large inventory position. In the first place, a sharp drop in price may cause serious losses; also, a large inventory may indicate that the company has accumulated a big supply of unsalable merchandise. The question still remains, however: *"What do we mean by large inventory?"*

As you certainly realize, an inventory is large or small only in terms of the yearly turnover and the type of business. We can discover the annual turnover of our sample company by dividing inventories (item 5) into total annual sales (item "a" on the income account).

It is also interesting to compare the value of the inventory of a company being studied with total current assets. Again, however, there is considerable variation between different types of companies, so that the relationship becomes significant only when compared with similar companies.

NET BOOK VALUE OF SECURITIES

There is one other very important thing that can be gotten from the balance sheet, and that is the net book or equity value of the company's securities. We can calculate the net book value of each of the three types of securities our company has outstanding by a little very simple arithmetic. *Book value means the value at which something is carried on the books of the company.*

The full rights of the bondholders come before any of the rights of the stockholders, so, to find the net book value or net tangible assets backing up the bonds we add together the balance sheet value of the bonds, preferred stock, common stock, reserve, and surplus. This gives us a total of $9,630,000. (We would not include contingency reserve if we were reasonably sure the contingency was going to arise, but, as general reserves are often equivalent to surplus, it is, usually, best to treat the reserve just as though it were surplus.) However, part of this value represents the goodwill and patents carried at $100,000, which is not a tangible item, so, to be conservative, we subtract this amount, leaving $9,530,000 as the total net book value of the bonds. This is equivalent to $4,765 for each $1,000 bond, a generous figure. To calculate the net book value of the preferred stock, we must eliminate the face value of the bonds, and then, following the same procedure, add the value of the preferred stock, common stock, reserve, and surplus, and subtract goodwill. This gives us a total net book value for the preferred stock of $7,530,000 or $753 for each share of $100 par value preferred. This is also very good coverage for the preferred stock, but we must examine current earnings before becoming too enthusiastic about the *value* of any security.

The net book value of the common stock, while an interesting figure, is not so important as the coverage on the senior securities. In case of liquidation, there is seldom much left for the common stockholders because of the normal loss in value of company assets when they are put up for sale, as mentioned before. The book value figure, however, does give us a basis for comparison with other companies. Comparisons of net book value over a period of years also show us if the company is a soundly growing one or, on the other hand, is losing ground. Earnings, however, are our important measure of common stock values, as we will see shortly.

The net book value of the common stock is found by adding the stated value of the common stock, reserves, and surplus and then subtracting patents and goodwill. This gives us a total net book value of $6,530,000. As there are 400,000 shares of common outstanding, each share has a net book value of $16.32. You must be careful not to be misled by book value figures, particularly of common stock. Profitable companies (Coca-Cola, for example) often show a very low net book value and very substantial earnings. Railroads, on the other hand, may show a high book value for their common stock but have such low or irregular earnings that the market price of the stock is much less than its apparent book value. Banks, insurance companies, and investment -trusts are exceptions to what we have said about common stock net book value. As their assets are largely liquid (i.e., cash, accounts receivable, and marketable securities), the book value of their common stock sometimes indicates its value very accurately.

PROPORTION OF BONDS, PREFERRED AND COMMON STOCK
Before investing, you will want to know the proportion of each kind of security issued by the company you are considering. A high proportion of bonds reduces the attractiveness of both the preferred and common stock, while too large an amount of preferred detracts from the value of the common.

The *bond ratio* is found by dividing the face value of the bonds (item 21), or $2,000,000, by the total value of the bonds, preferred stock, common stock, reserve, and surplus, or $9,630,000. This shows that bonds amount to about 20 per cent of the total of bonds, capital, and surplus.

The *preferred stock ratio* is found in the same way, only we divide the stated value of the preferred stock by the total of the other five items. Since we have half as much preferred stock as we have bonds, the preferred ratio is roughly 10.

Naturally, the *common stock ratio* will be the difference between 100 per cent and the totals of the bonds and preferred, or 70 per cent in our sample company. You will want to remember that the most valuable method of determining the common stock ratio is in combination with reserve and surplus. The surplus, as we have noted, is additional backing for the common stock and usually represents either original funds paid in to the company in excess of the stated value of the common stock (capital surplus), or undistributed earnings (earned surplus).

Most investment analysts carefully examine industrial companies that have more than about a quarter of their capitalization represented by bonds, while common stock should total at least as much as all senior securities (bonds and preferred issues). When this is not the case, companies often find it difficult to raise new capital. Banks don't like to lend them money because of the already large debt, and it is sometimes difficult to sell common stock because of all the bond interest or preferred dividends that must be paid before anything is available for the common stockholder.

Railroads and public utility companies are exceptions to most of the rules of thumb that we use in discussing The ABC Manufacturing Company, Inc. Their situation is different because of the tremendous amounts of money they have invested in their fixed assets., their small inventories and the ease with which they can collect their receivables. Senior securities of railroads and utility companies frequently amount to more than half of their capitalization. Speculators often interest themselves in companies that have a high proportion of debt or preferred stock because of the *leverage factor*. A simple illustration will show why. Let us take, for example, a company with $10,000,000 of 4 per cent bonds outstanding. If the company is earning $440,000 before bond interest, there will be only $40,000 left for the common stock ($10,000,000 at 4% equals $400,000). However, an increase of only 10 per cent in earnings (to $484,000) will leave $84,000 for common stock dividends, or an increase of more than 100 per cent. If there is only a small common issue, the increase in earnings per share would appear very impressive.

You have probably already noticed that a decline of 10 per cent in earnings would not only wipe out everything available for the common stock, but result in the company being unable to cover its full interest on its bonds without dipping into surplus. This is the great danger of so-called high leverage stocks and also illustrates the fundamental weakness of companies that have a disproportionate amount of debt or preferred stock. Investors would do well to steer clear of them. Speculators, however, will continue to be fascinated by the market opportunities they offer.

THE INCOME ACCOUNT

The fundamental soundness of a company, as shown by its balance sheet, is important to investors, but of even greater interest is the record of its operation. Its financial structure shows much of its ability to weather storms and pick up speed when times are good. It is the income record, however, that shows us how a company is actually doing and gives us our best guide to the future.

The *Consolidated Income and Earned Surplus* account of our company is stated on the next page. Follow the items given there and we will find out just how our company earned its money, what it did with its earnings, and what it all means in terms of our three classes of securities. We have used a combined income and surplus account because that is the form most frequently followed by industrial companies. However, sometimes the two statements are given separately. Also, a variety of names are used to describe this same part of the financial report. Sometimes it is called profit and loss account, sometimes *record of earnings,* and, often, simply *income account.* They are all the same thing.

The details that you will find on different income statements also vary a great deal. Some companies show only eight or ten separate items, while others will give a page or more of closely spaced entries that break down each individual type of revenue or cost. We have tried to strike a balance between extremes; give the major items that are in most income statements, omitting details that are only interesting to the expert analyst.

The most important source of revenue always makes up the first item on the income statement. In our company, it is *Net Sales* (item "a"). If it were a railroad or a utility instead of a manufacturer, this item would be called *gross revenues.* In any case, it represents the money paid into the company by its customers. Net sales are given to show that the figure represents the amount of money actually received after allowing for discounts and returned goods.

Net sales or gross revenues, you will note, is given before any kind of miscellaneous revenue that might have been received from investments, the sale of company property, tax refunds, or the like. A well-prepared income statement is always set up this way so that the stockholder can estimate the success of the company in fulfilling its major job of selling goods or service. If this were not so, you could not tell whether the company was really losing or making money on its operations, particularly over the last few years when tax rebates and other unusual things have often had great influence on final net income figures.

COST OF SALES

A general heading, *Cost of Sales, Expenses and Other Operating Charges* (item "b") is characteristic of a manufacturing company, but a utility company or railroad would call all of these things *operating expenses.*

The most important subdivision is *Cost of Goods Sold* (item "c"). Included under cost of goods sold are all of the expenses that go directly into the manufacture of the products the company sells -- raw materials, wages, freight, power, and rent. We have lumped these expenses together, as many companies do. Sometimes, however, you will find each item listed separately. Analyzing a detailed income account is a pretty technical operation and had best be left to the expert.

The ABC Manufacturing Company, Inc.
CONSOLIDATED INCOME AND EARNED SURPLUS
For the Year Ended December 31

Item
a.	Sales		$10,000,000
b.	COST OF SALES, EXPENSES AND OTHER OPERATING CHARGES:		
c.	Cost of Goods Sold	$7,000,000	
d.	Selling, Administrative & Gen. Expenses	500,000	
e.	Depreciation	200,000	
f.	Maintenance and Repairs	400,000	
g.	Taxes (Other than Federal Inc. Taxes)	300,000	8,400,000
h.	NET PROFIT FROM OPERATIONS		$ 1,600,000
i.	OTHER INCOME:		
j.	Royalties and Dividends	$ 250,000	
k.	Interest	25,000	275,000
l.	TOTAL		$ 1,875,000
m.	INTEREST CHARGES:		
n.	Interest on Funded Debt	$ 70,000	
o.	Other Interest	20,000	90,000
p.	NET INCOME BEFORE PROVISION FOR FED. INCOME TAXES		$ 1,785,000
q.	PROVISION FOR FEDERAL INCOME TAXES		678,300
r.	NET INCOME		$ 1,106,700
s.	DIVIDENDS:		
t.	Preferred Stock - $5.00 Per Share	$ 50,000	
u.	Common Stock - $1.00 Per Share	400,000	
v.	PROVISION FOR CONTINGENCIES	200,000	650,000
w.	BALANCE CARRIED TO EARNED SURPLUS		$ 456,700
x.	EARNED SURPLUS – JANUARY 1		3,073,000
y.	EARNED SURPLUS – DECEMBER 31		$ 3,530,000

We have shown separately, opposite "d," the *Selling, Administrative and General Expenses* of the past year. Unfortunately, there is little uniformity among companies in their treatment of these important non-manufacturing costs. Our figure includes the expenses of management; that is, executive salaries and clerical costs; commissions and salaries paid to salesmen; advertising expenses, and the like.

Depreciation ("e") shows us the amount that the company transferred from income during the year to the depreciation reserve that we ran across before as item "11" on the balance sheet (page 2). Depreciation must be charged against income unless the company is going to live on its own fat, something that no company can do for long and stay out of bankruptcy.

MAINTENANCE

Maintenance and Repairs (item "f") represents the money spent to keep the plant in good operating order. For example, the truck that we mentioned under depreciation must be kept running day by day. The cost of new tires, recharging the battery, painting and mechanical repairs are all maintenance costs. Despite this day-to-day work on the truck, the company must still provide for the time when it wears out -- hence, the reserve for depreciation.

You can readily understand from your own experience the close connection between maintenance and depreciation. If you do not take good care of your own car, you will have to buy a new one sooner than you would had you maintained it well. Corporations face the same problem with all of their equipment. If they do not do a good job of maintenance, much more will have to be set aside for depreciation to replace the abused tools and property.

Taxes are always with us. A profitable company always pays at least two types of taxes. One group of taxes are paid without regard to profits, and include real estate taxes, excise taxes, social security, and the like (item "g"). As these payments are a direct part of the cost of doing business, they must be included before we can determine the *Net Profit From Operations* (item "h").

Net Profit from Operations (sometimes called *gross profit)* tells us what the company made from manufacturing and selling its products. It is an interesting figure to investors because it indicates .how efficiently and successfully the company operates in its primary purpose as a creator of wealth. As a glance at the income account will tell you, there are still several other items to be deducted before the stockholder can hope to get anything. You can also easily imagine that for many companies these other items may spell the difference between profit and loss. For these reasons, we use net profit from operations as an indicator of progress in manufacturing and merchandising efficiency, not as a judge of the investment quality of securities.

Miscellaneous Income not connected with the major purpose of the company is generally listed after net profit from operations. There are quite a number of ways that corporations increase their income, including interest and dividends on securities they own, fees for special services performed, royalties on patents they allow others to use, and tax refunds. Our income statement shows *Other Income* as item "i," under which is shown income from *Royalties and Dividends* (item "j"), and, as a separate entry, *Interest* (item "k") which the company received from its bond investments. The *Total* of other income (item t1t?) shows us how much The ABC Manufacturing Company received from so-called *outside activities.* Corporations with diversified interests often receive tremendous amounts of *other income.*

INTEREST CHARGES

There is one other class of expenses that must be deducted from our income before we can determine the base on which taxes are paid, and that is *Interest Charges* (item "m"). As our company has $2,000,000 worth of 3 1/2 per cent bonds outstanding, it will pay *Interest on Funded Debt* of $70,000 (item "n"). During the year, the company also borrowed money from the bank, on which it, of course, paid interest, shown as *Other Interest* (item "o").

Net Income Before Provision for Federal Income Taxes (item "p") is an interesting figure for historical comparison. It shows us how profitable the company was in all of its various operations. A comparison of this entry over a period of years will enable you to see how well the company had been doing as a business institution before the Government stepped in for its share of net earnings. Federal taxes have varied so much in recent years that earnings before taxes are often a real help in judging business progress.

A few paragraphs back we mentioned that a profitable corporation pays two general types of taxes. We have already discussed those that are paid without reference to profits. *Provision for Federal Income Taxes* (item "q") is ordinarily figured on the total income of the company after normal business expenses, and so appears on our income account below these charges. Bond interest, for example, as it is payment on a loan, is deducted beforehand. Preferred and common stock dividends, which are *profits* that go to owners of the company, come after all charges and taxes.

NET INCOME

After we have deducted all of our expenses and income taxes from total income, we get *Net Income* (item "r"). Net income is the most interesting figure of all to the investor. Net income is the amount available to pay dividends on the preferred and common stock. From the balance sheet, we have learned a good deal about the company's stability and soundness of structure; from net profit from operations, we judge whether the company is improving in industrial efficiency. Net income tells us whether the securities of the company are likely to be a profitable investment.

The figure given for a single year is not nearly all of the story, however. As we have noted before, the historical record is usually more important than the figure for any given year. This is just as true of net income as any other item. So many things change from year to year that care must be taken not to draw hasty conclusions. During the war, Excess Profits Taxes had a tremendous effect on the earnings of many companies. In the next few years, *carryback tax credits* allowed some companies to show a net profit despite the fact that they had operated at a loss. Even net income can be a misleading figure unless one examines it carefully. A rough and easy way of judging how *sound* a figure it is would be to compare it with previous years.

The investor in stocks has a vital interest in *Dividends* (item "s"). The first dividend that our company must pay is that on its *Preferred Stock* (item "t"). Some companies will even pay preferred dividends out of earned surplus accumulated in the past if the net income is not large enough, but such a company is skating on thin ice unless the situation is most unusual.

The directors of our company decided to pay dividends totaling $400,000 on the *Common Stock,* or $1 a share (item "u"). As we have noted before, the amount of dividends paid is not determined by net income, but by a decision of the stockholders' representatives - the company's directors. Common dividends, just like preferred dividends, can be paid out of surplus if there is little or no net income. Sometimes companies do this if they have a long history of regular payments and don't want to spoil the record because of some special temporary situation that caused them to lose money. This occurs even less frequently and is more *dangerous* than paying preferred dividends out of surplus.

It is much more common, on the contrary, to *plough earnings back into the business* -- a phrase you frequently see on the financial pages and in company reports. The directors of our typical company have decided to pay only $1 on the common stock, though net income would have permitted them to pay much more. They decided that the company should *save* the difference.

The next entry on our income account, *Provision for Contingencies* (item "v"), shows us where our reserve for contingencies arose. The treasurer of our typical company has put the provision for contingencies after dividends. However, you will discover, if you look at very many financial reports, that it is sometimes placed above net income.

All of the net income that was not paid out as dividends, or set aside for contingencies, is shown as *Balance Carried to Earned Surplus* (item "w"). In other words, it is kept in the business. In previous years, the company had also earned more than it paid out so it had already accumulated by the beginning of the year an earned surplus of $3,073,000 (item "x"). When we total the earned surplus accumulated during the year to that which the company had at the first of the year, we get the total earned surplus at the end' of the year (item "y"). You will notice that the total here is the same as that which we ran across on the balance sheet as item 27.

Not all companies combine their income and surplus account. When they do not, you will find that *balance carried to surplus will* be the last item on the income account. The statement of consolidated surplus would appear as a third section of the corporation's financial report. A separate surplus account might be used if the company shifted funds for reserves to surplus during the year or made any other major changes in its method of treating the surplus account.

ANALYZING THE INCOME ACCOUNT

The income account, like the balance sheet, will tell us a lot more if we make a few detailed comparisons. The size of the totals on an income account doesn't mean much by itself. A company can have hundreds of millions of dollars in net sales and be a very bad investment. On the other hand, even a very modest profit in round figures may make a security attractive if there are only a small number of shares outstanding.

Before you select a company for investment, you will want to know something of its *margin of profit,* and how this figure has changed over the years. Finding the margin of profit is very simple. We just divide the net profit from operations (item "h") by net sales (item "a"). The figure we get (0.16) shows us that the company make a profit of 16 per cent from operations. By itself, though, this is not very helpful. We can make it significant in two ways.

In the first place, we can compare it with the margin of profit in previous years, and, from this comparison, learn if the company excels other companies that do a similar type of business. If the margin of profit of our company is very low in comparison with other companies in the same field, it is an unhealthy sign. Naturally, if it is high, we have grounds to be optimistic.

Analysts also frequently use *operating ratio* for the same purpose. The operating ratio is the complement of the margin of profit. The margin of profit of our typical company is 16. The operating ratio is 84. You can find the operating ratio either by subtracting the margin of profit from 100 or dividing the total of operating costs ($8,400,000) by net sales ($10,000,000).

The margin of profit figure and the operating ratio, like all of those ratios we examined in connection with the balance sheet, give us general information about the company, help us judge its prospects for the future. All of these comparisons have significance for the long term as they tell us about the fundamental economic condition of the company. But you still have the right to ask: *"Are the securities good investments for me now?"*

Investors, as opposed to speculators, are primarily interested in two things. The first is safety for their capital and the second, regularity of income. They are also interested in the rate of return on their investment but, as you will see, the rate of return will be affected by the importance placed on safety and regularity. High income implies risk. Safety must be bought by accepting a lower return.

The safety of any security is determined primarily by the earnings of the company that are available to pay interest or dividends on the particular issue. Again, though, round dollar figures aren't of much help to us. What we want to know is the relationship between the total money available and the requirements for each of the securities issued by the company.

INTEREST COVERAGE

As the bonds of our company represent part of its debt, the first thing we want to know is how easily the company can pay the interest. From the income account we see that the company had total income of $1,875,000 (item "1"). The interest charge on our bonds each year is $70,000 (3 1/2 per cent of $2,000,000 - item 21 on the balance sheet). Dividing total income by bond interest charges ($1,875,000 by $70,000) shows us that the company earned its bond interest 26 times over. Even after income taxes, bond interest was earned 17 times, a method of testing employed by conservative analysts. Before an industrial bond should be considered a safe investment, most analysts say that the company should earn interest charges several times over, so our company has a wide margin of safety.

To calculate the *preferred dividend coverage* (i.e., the number of times preferred dividends were earned), we must use net income as our base, as Federal Income Taxes and all interest charges must be paid before anything is available for stockholders. As we have 10,000 shares of $100 par value of preferred stock which pays a dividend of 5 per cent, the total dividend requirement for the preferred stock is $50,000 (items 24 on the balance sheet and "t" on the income account).

EARNINGS PER COMMON SHARE

The buyer of common stocks is often more concerned with the earnings per share of his stock than he is with the dividend. It is usually earnings per share or, rather, prospective earnings per share, that influence stock market prices. Our income account does not show the earnings available for the common stock, so we must calculate it ourselves. It is net income less preferred dividends (items "r" - "t"), or $1,056,700. From the balance sheet, we know that there are 400,000 shares outstanding, so the company earned about $2.64 per share.

All of these ratios have been calculated for a single year. It cannot be emphasized too strongly, however, that the *record* is more important to the investor than the report of any single year. By all the tests we have employed, both the bonds and the preferred stock of our typical company appear to be very good investments,, if their market prices were not too high. The investor would want to look back, however, to determine whether the operations were reasonably typical of the company.

Bonds and preferred stocks that are very safe usually sell at pretty high prices, so the yield to the investor is small. For example, if our company has been showing about the same coverage on its preferred dividends for many years and there is good reason to believe that the future will be equally kind, the company would probably replace the old 5 per cent preferred with a new issue paying a lower rate, perhaps 4 per cent.

STOCK PRICES

As the common stock does not receive a guaranteed dividend, its market value is determined by a great variety of influences in addition to the present yield of the stock measured by its dividends. The stock market, by bringing together buyers and sellers from all over the world, reflects their composite judgment of the present and future value of the stock. We cannot attempt here to write a treatise on the stock market. There is one important ratio, however, that every common stock buyer considers. That is the ratio of earnings to market price.

The so-called *price-earnings ratio is* simply the earnings per share on the common stock divided into the market price. Our typical company earned $2.64 a common share in the year, If the stock were selling at $30 a share, its price-earnings ratio would be about 11.4. This is the basic figure that you would want to use in comparing the common stock of this particular company with other similar stocks.

IMPORTANT TERMS AND CONCEPTS

LIABILITIES
WHAT THE COMPANY OWES -- + RESERVES + SURPLUS + STOCKHOLDERS INTEREST IN THE COMPANY

ASSETS
WHAT THE COMPANY OWNS -- + WHAT IS OWED TO THE COMPANY

FIXED ASSETS
MACHINERY, EQUIPMENT, BUILDINGS, ETC.

EXAMPLES OF FIXED ASSETS
DESKS, TABLES, FILING CABINETS, BUILDINGS, LAND, TIMBERLAND, CARS AND TRUCKS, LOCOMOTIVES AND FREIGHT CARS, SHIPYARDS, OIL LANDS, ORE DEPOSITS, FOUNDRIES

EXAMPLES OF:
PREPAID EXPENSES
PREPAID INSURANCE, PREPAID RENT, PREPAID ROYALTIES AND PREPAID INTEREST

DEFERRED CHARGES
AMORTIZATION OF BOND DISCOUNT, ORGANIZATION EXPENSE, MOVING EXPENSES, DEVELOPMENT EXPENSES

ACCOUNTS PAYABLE
BILLS THE COMPANY OWES TO OTHERS

BONDHOLDERS ARE CREDITORS
BOND CERTIFICATES ARE IOU'S ISSUED BY A COMPANY BACKED BY A PLEDGE

BONDHOLDERS ARE OWNERS
A STOCK CERTIFICATE IS EVIDENCE OF THE SHAREHOLDER'S OWNERSHIP

EARNED SURPLUS
INCOME PLOWED BACK INTO THE BUSINESS

NET SALES
GROSS SALES MINUS DISCOUNTS AND RETURNED GOODS

NET INCOME
= TOTAL INCOME MINUS ALL EXPENSES AND INCOME TAXES

ANSWER SHEET

USE THE SPECIAL PENCIL.   MAKE GLOSSY BLACK MARKS.

	A	B	C	D	E		A	B	C	D	E		A	B	C	D	E		A	B	C	D	E		A	B	C	D	E
1	::	::	::	::	::	26	::	::	::	::	::	51	::	::	::	::	::	76	::	::	::	::	::	101	::	::	::	::	::
2	::	::	::	::	::	27	::	::	::	::	::	52	::	::	::	::	::	77	::	::	::	::	::	102	::	::	::	::	::
3	::	::	::	::	::	28	::	::	::	::	::	53	::	::	::	::	::	78	::	::	::	::	::	103	::	::	::	::	::
4	::	::	::	::	::	29	::	::	::	::	::	54	::	::	::	::	::	79	::	::	::	::	::	104	::	::	::	::	::
5	::	::	::	::	::	30	::	::	::	::	::	55	::	::	::	::	::	80	::	::	::	::	::	105	::	::	::	::	::
6	::	::	::	::	::	31	::	::	::	::	::	56	::	::	::	::	::	81	::	::	::	::	::	106	::	::	::	::	::
7	::	::	::	::	::	32	::	::	::	::	::	57	::	::	::	::	::	82	::	::	::	::	::	107	::	::	::	::	::
8	::	::	::	::	::	33	::	::	::	::	::	58	::	::	::	::	::	83	::	::	::	::	::	108	::	::	::	::	::
9	::	::	::	::	::	34	::	::	::	::	::	59	::	::	::	::	::	84	::	::	::	::	::	109	::	::	::	::	::
10	::	::	::	::	::	35	::	::	::	::	::	60	::	::	::	::	::	85	::	::	::	::	::	110	::	::	::	::	::

Make only ONE mark for each answer.   Additional and stray marks may be counted as mistakes.   In making corrections, erase errors COMPLETELY.

	A	B	C	D	E		A	B	C	D	E		A	B	C	D	E		A	B	C	D	E		A	B	C	D	E
11	::	::	::	::	::	36	::	::	::	::	::	61	::	::	::	::	::	86	::	::	::	::	::	111	::	::	::	::	::
12	::	::	::	::	::	37	::	::	::	::	::	62	::	::	::	::	::	87	::	::	::	::	::	112	::	::	::	::	::
13	::	::	::	::	::	38	::	::	::	::	::	63	::	::	::	::	::	88	::	::	::	::	::	113	::	::	::	::	::
14	::	::	::	::	::	39	::	::	::	::	::	64	::	::	::	::	::	89	::	::	::	::	::	114	::	::	::	::	::
15	::	::	::	::	::	40	::	::	::	::	::	65	::	::	::	::	::	90	::	::	::	::	::	115	::	::	::	::	::
16	::	::	::	::	::	41	::	::	::	::	::	66	::	::	::	::	::	91	::	::	::	::	::	116	::	::	::	::	::
17	::	::	::	::	::	42	::	::	::	::	::	67	::	::	::	::	::	92	::	::	::	::	::	117	::	::	::	::	::
18	::	::	::	::	::	43	::	::	::	::	::	68	::	::	::	::	::	93	::	::	::	::	::	118	::	::	::	::	::
19	::	::	::	::	::	44	::	::	::	::	::	69	::	::	::	::	::	94	::	::	::	::	::	119	::	::	::	::	::
20	::	::	::	::	::	45	::	::	::	::	::	70	::	::	::	::	::	95	::	::	::	::	::	120	::	::	::	::	::
21	::	::	::	::	::	46	::	::	::	::	::	71	::	::	::	::	::	96	::	::	::	::	::	121	::	::	::	::	::
22	::	::	::	::	::	47	::	::	::	::	::	72	::	::	::	::	::	97	::	::	::	::	::	122	::	::	::	::	::
23	::	::	::	::	::	48	::	::	::	::	::	73	::	::	::	::	::	98	::	::	::	::	::	123	::	::	::	::	::
24	::	::	::	::	::	49	::	::	::	::	::	74	::	::	::	::	::	99	::	::	::	::	::	124	::	::	::	::	::
25	::	::	::	::	::	50	::	::	::	::	::	75	::	::	::	::	::	100	::	::	::	::	::	125	::	::	::	::	::

ANSWER SHEET

TEST NO. _____ PART _____ TITLE OF POSITION _____

PLACE OF EXAMINATION _____ DATE _____

(CITY OR TOWN)　　　　　　　　　　　　　　(STATE)

RATING

USE THE SPECIAL PENCIL.　MAKE GLOSSY BLACK MARKS.

	A B C D E		A B C D E		A B C D E		A B C D E		A B C
1		26		51		76		101	
2		27		52		77		102	
3		28		53		78		103	
4		29		54		79		104	
5		30		55		80		105	
6		31		56		81		106	
7		32		57		82		107	
8		33		58		83		108	
9		34		59		84		109	
10		35		60		85		110	

Make only ONE mark for each answer.　Additional and stray marks may be
counted as mistakes.　In making corrections, erase errors COMPLETELY.

	A B C D E		A B C D E		A B C D E		A B C D E		A B C
11		36		61		86		111	
12		37		62		87		112	
13		38		63		88		113	
14		39		64		89		114	
15		40		65		90		115	
16		41		66		91		116	
17		42		67		92		117	
18		43		68		93		118	
19		44		69		94		119	
20		45		70		95		120	
21		46		71		96		121	
22		47		72		97		122	
23		48		73		98		123	
24		49		74		99		124	
				75		100		125	